AF272046

Julie von Bismarck

With the horse, not on the horse

A guide to fine riding

Publisher's imprint

Julie von Bismarck
With the horse, not on the horse - A guide to fine riding
ISBN: 978-3-9822821-9-0
Originally published in German as "*Mit dem Pferd statt auf dem Pferd -
Ein Leitfaden für feines Reiten*"
ISBN: 978-3-9820414-9-0
Copyright Julie von Bismarck
1st edition, paperback published 2019
English translation: Sue Anderson for Anima Translation
Cover design: author
Printer: BoD
Self-published by Verlag von Bismarck
Julie von Bismarck
Herrenholz 18
23556 Lübeck
Illustrations: private; photographs: istock photo
This work, including all parts hereof, is protected by copyright. Any use outside the narrow limits of copyright law is prohibited unless with the author's consent. This applies in particular to any electronic or other form of reproduction, translation, distribution or public dissemination.
Printed in Germany, Canada, USA, Australia

I would like to thank all the horses I have met in my life, who have taught me so much.
Special thanks go to my horse and best friend Summer, who showed me a whole new level of finesse and easy communication.

I also want to thank my late grandmother, who taught me how to listen to horses and who left me the wonderful exercises in this book. Although I have altered them a bit, the basic ideas are the ones she taught me.

Chapter 1

In over forty years as a rider, I have ridden every possible type of horse: lazy, fizzy, bolting, bucking, rearing, naughty, stubborn, timid.

Horses that were hard to flex and bend or, at the opposite extreme, were always bent and couldn't be straightened. Horses that were hard to get on the bit, or that went on the bit immediately at the lightest touch on the reins.

Horses that spooked constantly, were always in a state of high alert, and panicked at the slightest provocation.

What I soon realised, however, was that precisely these descriptions as "lazy", "fizzy", "sluggish", "timid" or "stiff" were doing the horses an injustice. Because there's a reason for every behaviour.

In the opinion of my grandmother, on whose farm I learned to ride, the reason always lay solely and squarely with the rider.

In her eyes there were no bad or good horses, there were only good or bad riders.

It was under this maxim that we learned how to handle horses and how to actually ride. In practice, that meant that there were rules for everything, even for fetching a horse from the pasture, and if you had to run after your horse to catch it, you'd done something wrong.

When horses I was leading pulled me across the path to reach an especially tempting tuft of grass, when they bucked on an outride, or took a huge leap sideways to avoid an invisible danger, or when anything else went wrong, I always saw this as evidence that I hadn't understood yet the nature of horses well enough to be able to handle them as calmly and easily as my grandmother did – and that I definitely couldn't yet count myself as a good rider.

My grandmother explained to us in very clear and visual terms precisely how to do things with the horse, but then essentially she just left us to practise.

It was a school I wouldn't have exchanged for anything, because it was this direct experience – seeing the consequences of your own mistakes first-hand and feeling the elation when you did it differently the next time and it worked out – that led automatically to a deep, fundamental feeling and understanding for horses that might otherwise have been hard to achieve. At least at such a young age.

My grandmother didn't think much of "aids" such as sharp bits. The only thing she used occasionally with us not-quite-so-good-yet riders were the good old leather side-reins buckled to the girth, that were always kept long.

She was convinced that any horse could be ridden and controlled by seat alone – provided you had the stamina to cope with the necessary disciplined schooling of the rider.

In those days, the rider's schooling came at the expense of the rider, not the horse. In other words, the rider had to learn to communicate with the horse and keep working on their skills.

There was never any question of compensating for a lack of riding ability by reaching for a sharp bit or allowing coercion and force.

On our farm, it was the *rider* who suffered, not the horse. *We* were the ones with the scraped knees and aching bones after falling off and remounting for the third time.

I must admit that I didn't always enjoy this kind of schooling either, nor did I always share my grandmother's opinion.

For example, each time I found myself on one of her thoroughbreds (rescued from the racetrack as unrideable, who invariably bolted with me on every ride and not only totally ignored me but also seemed completely immune to any influence on my part) and hurtling towards a sharp turn, I would already visualise myself lying under the overturned horse or plastered against the nearest pine tree, and I would curse her stoic composure and wish for nothing more than a Pelham.

Today I can laugh about it because I know that, in reality, I was very lucky to learn to ride in that way. Simply because we are naturally shaped by the way we are taught.

Without all of those falls, those bolting thoroughbreds, that stubborn pony, the giant straight-necked Hanoverians that could easily take 90 minutes to get on the bit, not to mention the crazy Trakehners whose oversized droopy ears always deceived you into believing they were even-tempered, only to morph in the blink of an eye into overwrought bundles of nerves and then, seconds later, into daredevil superheroes who – without asking me – would throw themselves straight down the next slope at breakneck speed.

Without all these different horses and all these experiences, I would have missed out on a lot of insights that I believe are important for a rider.

One of these was that riding is basically dangerous to begin with. Falling off is part of it (and can never be avoided completely, no matter how well you ride). There's always a risk of an accidental head-butt or having a rope dragged through your hand. Or a great lump of horse that will serenely and matter-of-factly rest its full weight right on your foot, protected only by a lightweight summer shoe, look at you as if butter wouldn't melt when you yell at it to take its hoof off your foot at once, then calmly shift a bit more of its weight onto the hoof in question.

Another insight was that riding didn't seem to be as dangerous for my grandmother as it was for me. No horse ever stepped on her foot, she never got head-butted, no horse ever pulled the rope through her hand – on the contrary, every single horse treated her with the utmost respect, took care not to harm her, and would probably have plucked a piece of lint from her riding jacket if they could have.

Watching this was, I think, an equally important experience for me: seeing how a horse – the same horse who, every time I groomed and saddled him, would shift to and fro until he found a foot to stand on while snorting in contentment; who, when having his hooves picked, would take me five minutes per leg until he felt comfortable enough to lift the hoof by precisely one millimetre so I could barely see the sole; who clenched his mouth when I tried to bridle him and was clearly already devising ways to annoy me on the ride; who, in short, did everything he could to make my life as a rider more difficult – behaved with my grandmother.

The same horse stood beside her like a statue, moved aside politely at her tiniest signal, lifted all four hooves for her to pick (so high that it looked unnatural) and happily let himself be saddled and bridled, with an expression of joyful expectation on his face.

This was true of every horse and it was true not only in handling but also in riding.

Every single one of these horses, who with me essentially acted up and made my life as a rider difficult, were instantly transformed under my grandmother into radiant, contented, laid-back specimens and 100% loyal partners.

My grandmother could ride the most difficult of

horses; it always looked so easy, as if she and the horse were communicating through thoughts alone.

It always seemed to me as if the pair were in a dialogue, a conversation between two friends, and you never noticed her giving any aids.

The reins were always a bit "too long" if anything, and I never saw my grandmother pull on a horse's mouth, hit a horse, or treat one roughly in any other way – she was just as kind and polite to the horses as they were to her.

However, I also never met anyone who rode so often and for so long with the stirrups crossed in front of the saddle, who worked so hard on their seat and their own riding fitness, and was so utterly disciplined.

So this was the key insight: the reason why riding was more dangerous for me, why the horses were so "difficult", "naughty", "hard-mouthed", "lazy" or "fizzy" under me and immediately seemed so easy and simple to ride with my grandmother in the saddle, was quite simple:

My grandmother had gained these horses' respect and affection though her kind, determined and competent handling, through the fact that she understood the essence of the horse. And the fact that she could ride.

Unlike me.

This insight spurred me on to learn everything there was to know about horses and to work on my riding skills with the utmost dedication.

Over the many years I've spent trying to get closer to this goal, one insight has become especially clear to me again and again in a wide variety of situations: handling and riding horses cannot be about subduing or controlling the horse; riding in its positive form can only succeed if the rider is able to gain the horse's trust and build up a genuine friendship with it. Which involves listening and talking to it – talking as kindly as you would to your best friend, in a language the horse can understand – to rule out misunderstandings as far as possible.

Riding is about finding a reliable friend and partner in the horse, one who voluntarily works and thinks with you and contributes to your successes.

It also became very clear time and again that, while it's true you can make a horse docile by using coercion, force and painful tack, this inflicts damage on a scale that goes far beyond physical pain – and that the horse never forgets this.

This is of course a good way to make enemies, but definitely no basis for a friendly, harmonious partnership and certainly no way to gain a horse as a friend.

So I set out to look for ways to gain a horse's trust and respect.

At the time, I had a foster pony who was both "dull" and loutish. I was allowed to ride him a couple of times a week while I was at school in town, and this pony now became my test subject.

Riding this pony was a dangerous and frustrating experience every time, because he couldn't be steered, didn't respond to leg aids and generally gave the impression that he thought very little of riding or of me as a person. Getting this pony into the desired gait or making him obey, turn or halt was a feat of strength for me every time and, to be honest, not much fun.

He would graciously deign to eat the treats that I'd spent all of my pocket money on – but that was about it.

One day once again (for what must have been the hundredth time), the pony bolted on the way back after a hack and raced at full tilt between two closely spaced trees, aiming to brush me off.

I remember realising exactly what he was planning and hauling on the reins with all my might in order to turn him. But no chance. His plan worked and led to me dragging myself the two miles back to the stable with a broken tibia. (Yes, I was allowed to ride out on my own even as a child and teenager.)

So this pony wasn't really rideable and in a sense he was even dangerous but it was precisely this that made him an ideal candidate to find out if obvious antipathy could be turned into friendship or at least into interest by taking a different approach.

As an experiment, I decided to play with the pony. And so, instead of riding, I stuffed my pockets with bags of treats, walked him to an empty meadow, took off his halter and tried to get him to follow me.

My idea was this: if he follows me willingly, maybe he'll listen to me better while riding.

As soon as I'd taken off the halter, the pony plunged his nose into the grass with relish, completely ignoring me and my treats.

I spent the rest of that day's stable time trying to catch the halterless pony in the wide open meadow, a task that I finally achieved only with a bucket of oats. This first attempt had therefore turned out more of a bitter disappointment than a resounding success – but I wasn't going to throw in the towel so quickly.

Maybe I should have started in a sandy arena with no lush grass, I reasoned – and that's exactly what I did on my next try.

After the first experience with my "confidence-building measure", however, I wasn't especially optimistic that this time would be any different.

So I was amazed and moved when the pony not only followed me with interest, but within minutes would trot when I trotted, canter when I cantered, and halt when I halted. I couldn't stop beaming, and for the first time I felt something like a real relationship with this horse. It was the first time in months that the pony didn't just ignore me or brush me off, but actually interacted with me.

For the next few weeks, I confined myself to this

kind of activity and communication, and soon he was following me without a halter, even across the yard and into the stable; in fact, he would even come running across the meadow when he saw me. I was overjoyed.

And this joy knew no bounds when I finally rode him again for the first time, because my hopes were exceeded: for the first time, I could ride anywhere and in any gait, the pony snorted contentedly and responded not only to the finest of aids but even to my thoughts. After dismounting, I hung around the pony's neck for a good half an hour, crying into his mane.

With happiness. The poor animal.

This was the first time in my life that I truly realised deep down how little is needed in order to communicate with a horse – and that anything beyond that makes the relationship more difficult rather than better.

Of course, I was still miles away from my grandmother's level of riding ability, but I understood then that I hadn't been wrong about the image that always came to mind when I saw her riding: horses respond even to thoughts – as long as they are not forced to switch off due to constant, exaggerated and usually unrefined "aid giving" (communication).

This is very important to know when talking about fine riding.

The rider makes the mistakes.

This basic rule holds true and it often boils down

to distraction on the part of the rider.

Controlling their own thoughts is therefore just as important for a rider as controlling their body.
Which sounds a lot simpler than it is.
I'm sure it's happened to most riders: your thoughts are on something other than the aids, and the horse responds to those thoughts while you yourself are still making the decision.
For example, during flying changes, when you think about the next change too early and the horse has already changed while you are still trying to concentrate and keep count.
Or when you're riding a course and think about taking a short-cut, but then decide to go for the longer route after all – and the horse has long since made the turn. So many times while cantering through the forest in cross-country, I've decided to ride to the left past a tree and at the last moment switched to go right instead – my horse and I often came to an abrupt standstill: right in the middle, face up against the tree trunk. All of this happens due to the rider's lack of concentration. All of this is our fault. Not the horse's.
The horse responds to the rider's body, thoughts and moods – so it's not his fault if the signals coming from there are unclear or conflicting. The rider should definitely have internalised this lesson.
It's not the horse that is lazy, sluggish, fizzy or unrideable, but the rider who hasn't yet found the right way to communicate with the horse so that he becomes a happy and willing partner.

The vast majority of the physical and psychological abnormalities I've seen in horses over the course of my career as an equine osteopath and acupuncturist have been the result of incorrect riding, painful tack and equipment and the effects of stress and overwork. They simply wouldn't have occurred without the horses' riders.

So that raises the question, what's going wrong? And one answer is pretty much this:

Even though I was largely saved from being unfair to horses by the way my grandmother treated her own animals, I still had horses that for simplicity I described as "lazy", "sluggish", "hard-mouthed" or "unmotivated". But most riders don't learn to ride in the way I was lucky enough to learn. By no means always because it's too much work and demands too much discipline, but often simply because so many riding instructors in recent decades have taught that riding is primarily about control over the horse, that this is best achieved via the reins and the horse's mouth, and that the primary sign of successful riding is therefore a round, deep neck with its nose as close as possible to the horse´s chest. Many riders have been taught to believe it makes them a good rider if they can hold the horse's head in this position and ride it like this through the gaits, paces and exercises and over the jumps that the rider wants.

Yes, this is certainly a posture in which the horse won't put up much resistance.

Because it can't see anything, because it's in pain and under considerable mental and physical tension, and because it can hardly breathe. Control is guaranteed – but it has nothing to do with real riding.

As the vast majority of people want to learn to ride because they love horses, this situation is especially deplorable: these riders would never harm their horses intentionally, so it's a tragedy when they do precisely that due to these learned attitudes.

If a rider fails to consider that there might be the reason for the problems with the horse, it starts a series of injustices that sometimes cause enormous harm.

Many riders see it as perfectly normal to label a horse as "unrideable", "sluggish", "moody" or "hard-mouthed" and then reach for sharper bits, draw-reins, longer spurs and whips, and "just push on with it" rather than looking for the cause – and they certainly don't start with themselves.

If these riders knew what they were doing to their horse in just one moment of injustice, they would leap off its back in horror, take off its bridle, and never ride again until they found another way.

The exercises in this book have helped me to achieve easy and sophisticated communication with many horses in my life that were seen as "difficult", so I hope they can help many other riders as well. After all, an easy, friendly style of fine riding is quite rightly what most of us strive for – because it's so much more enjoyable and maintains the horse's well-being.

The full consequences of an attitude where riders resort to methods and equipment that harm the horse rather than working on their own skills only became clear to me when I was confronted daily, in my work as an equine osteopath and acupuncturist, with injuries, pain and mistakes that were inflicted on horses by their riders and owners and were at the root of the poor animals' supposed laziness, naughtiness or unrideability.

And this was in every kind of horse, from across the full spectrum of equestrianism, in countries all over the world. (Read more in *Connections in the horse*)

The cases all had one thing in common:

With no exaggeration, most of the blockages, injuries, diseases and damages were caused by excessive force applied to the horse's head. By reins, bits, bitless bridles, lead-ropes or the like.

The fear of losing control, that is apparently widespread among riders and owners, was clearly the most common cause of pain and injury in the horse. And for most riders, control seemed to be guaranteed by exerting excessive force on the horse's head, face and mouth. The more "difficult" the horse, the more painful the tack used, and the more coercive measures such as Rollkur/LDR were applied.

With dire consequences for the misunderstood horses...

Fig. I: Use of the curb bit as a substitute for schooling

Fig. II: Lead-ropes/chains cutting into the gums above the incisors and the horse's lower jaw – control by inflicting pain

Fig. III: Wire bit and forced "LDR" / "Rollkur" posture

In my work as an equine osteopath, I saw horses described by their riders as "stiff, won't flex" that had had the corners of their mouths torn open from the inside.

Horses labelled as skittish and stubborn that were suffering from massive blockages and inflammation around the upper cervical joints and related muscle tension, as well as the migraine-like headaches that were very likely the result. (As everyone has probably experienced, when you're in pain your tolerance to stress goes down. A horse that suddenly seems more "skittish" or "highly strung" may simply be in pain.

I've often seen such horses suddenly revert to being calmness personified after the problems were treated, so I would assume that pain is one of the primary causes of a sudden increase in skittishness.)

I saw horses described as "crooked" that were "rounded" and lunged for hours on end, and finally turned out to have spavin (a degenerative, inflammatory condition of the hock joints), which was the cause of the horse's "crookedness".

I saw horses that clearly didn't want to canter, but were forced into it with whips and spurs. Horses in which I then found tendon damage, inflamed joints or severe blockages in the neck, shoulder or carpus – the reason for their refusal to canter.

And time and again I saw riders punishing their

horses for their own fears. For many horses, turning an ear back towards the rider led to their head immediately being yanked down into their chest and at the same time the spurs being sunk into their sides.

Horses with a history of bolting were ridden with the most painful types of bridle to hold them back. – Horses that had not had any physical limitations, but had never learned to trust the rider and should have been started from scratch with the absolute basics...

All of these situations were originally due to rider error, and were only made worse by the riders' responses. The health of these horses suffered due to their riders' anxiety and lack of knowledge and skill. Their health suffered because these riders didn't understand that riding doesn't mean sitting on a horse and controlling it.

They hadn't grasped the fact that riding is only *not* at the horse's expense if it is interpreted in the way that it should be: as a friendly partnership with the horse that requires constant communication.

It is possible to refine the rider-horse partnership in such a way that the horse can be ridden with minimal aids and without reins. This doesn't mean foregoing the reins entirely – it just means not relying on them as the rider's sole instrument of control.

It is possible to create such a reliable mutual understanding with the horse that you can communicate solely through thoughts and the tiniest of aids that occur automatically in the body. There's no need to switch to a neck ring for this, or to a bitless bridle (without levers) – but the beauty of it is that you *could*.

Which certainly doesn't mean you'll never find yourself on a bolting or bucking horse again, of course you will. And there will always be situations in which you have to handle a horse differently *at first* in order not to endanger yourself, the horse or third parties.
But if you and your horse manage to acquire the feel for riding that I hope to bring across in this book, your view of the horse and your own riding ability will change fundamentally.

I've been riding for over fourty years using the exercises and necessary inner attitude described in this book, and in that time I've experienced the most amazing effects and transformations in every possible type of horse.
It's impressive to see how supposedly "leg-dead" horses that have been forced round riding arenas for months or even years with constant kicking and flicks of the whip suddenly start to listen and canter with the lightest of aids or transition to an extended trot.
How fizzy horses that are always in a hurry suddenly let go, drop their necks, snort and focus on the rider with ears pointing forwards, backwards or to the side in turn.

How panicked, abused horses regain trust and are happy to see you.
How eagerly horses want to cooperate, and how much fun riding suddenly becomes.

As with everything in riding, it takes time and patience and real, solid concentration on seemingly tiny things. But I firmly believe that every rider and every horse can benefit from these guidelines and improve their partnership with the aid of the exercises explained here.

With this in mind, let's now turn to the basics of refining our communication with the horse, starting with the most obvious one, which is often also the most under-appreciated: our actual interaction with the horse.

Chapter 2

Riding was originally regarded not as a sport but as an art, and this term captures the essence of riding much better.

We've just addressed the fact that riding is not about power and control, but actually about focus, thoughts and communication. Because horses are so big and strong, many people seem to find it hard to imagine how sensitive these huge herbivores are.

Many riders believe they have to ride their horses with sharp bits, buckle the noseband as tightly as possible, pull on the mouth, and use coercive techniques such as LDR to control their half-tonne of concentrated horsepower.

This is a fatal mistake. A mistake that causes lasting psychological and physical damage to horses, often ending with fatal consequences.

This simply shouldn't happen.

So let's try to imagine this:

The horse is a highly sensitive animal that constantly picks up, interprets and responds to even the tiniest emotional fluctuations in the living creatures around it. Which of course includes those in the rider. The horse can chase away a tiny mosquito from anywhere on its vast expanse of coat with a precise twitch of the area concerned, because the surface of its skin is packed with receptors and nerve endings, giving it a sophisticated system of impulse transmission throughout its body.

The said mosquito is so light that a human being wouldn't even notice it on their skin; however, the horse can not only sense it, but also locate it precisely and chase it away with a well-aimed twitch. This seemingly mundane fact alone should make it clear to all that the horse is not an unfeeling fighting machine, but a highly sensitive mammal.

One of the few mammals, by the way, that cannot express pain through sound.

So as riders we need to be aware that sharp items of equipment, painful bridles, all of those thin rope halters and jagged spurs, create the exact response in the horse that they were designed for: pain.

The reason we can control a horse better with a rope halter is because it is more uncomfortable or more painful than a plain one.

The horse responds to the spur because it inflicts pain. The horse is "easier on the bit" with a sharp bit because it digs into its tongue, gums and lower jaw, causing significant pain which it tries to escape by lowering its head to avoid or at least relieve the pressure.

There are always other ways, so every rider has the choice. And anyone who still resorts to these methods and items of equipment should at least be aware that they are inflicting pain on their horse – and that this is the sole reason why these items "work".

Riding is about the tiniest of tiny things. A teeny bit more tension in a thigh, a calf shifted just a centimetre further back, a twist of a shoulder – all of this immediately sends a different signal to the horse and therefore produces a different response. This is precisely why absolute concentration and body control in the rider, as well as the ability to centre and focus their thoughts, is one of the key basic requirements for fine riding.

Which it was in the past, by the way:
The first people to use horses for riding and driving were soldiers and farmers.
Both soldiers at war and farmers working in the fields relied on communicating with their horses as effortlessly as possible and being able to trust them one hundred percent.
The farmer in the fields had too many other things to do without wasting time and effort manoeuvring his horses: he had to push the plough into the soil or load the hay or throw potatoes into the furrows, and he depended on his horses responding immediately to his voice commands and gestures, i.e. halting, walking on or turning.

Fig. IV: No hand free to control the mouth –
working with rather than against the horse

It was the same for the soldier, whose real task was not riding but fighting – for which he needed at least one hand free. For the soldier, perfect communication with his horse could be the deciding factor between life and death.

A soldier who had to pull his horse into every turn or drive the spurs into its flanks to make it canter in the heat of battle would probably not have survived very long.

Coordination with the horse therefore had to be as fine, as fast and as natural as possible.

To make sure this worked in an emergency, the schooling of horse and rider took up by far the majority of their time. Many years of carefully devised and sequenced exercises were the basic schooling for every aspiring rider and horse.

The goal was to achieve the best possible physical health of the horse and the finest possible understanding and 100% trust between horse and rider – and the fact that this could only be achieved through extraordinary skill and self-control on the part of the rider was completely self-evident.

During all those years of training, therefore, it was mainly the rider who was drilled and not the horse.

If you look at the extremely demanding exercises that riders had to do in the past, even in basic schooling, it comes as no surprise that today's riders so often lack fearlessness, balance and skill.

Fig. V: Complete trust on both sides – the horse as comrade

Standing on a bare horse (in the wild, with no bridle, halter, etc.), leaping onto the horse without aids, getting the horse to retrieve, like a dog, getting the unhaltered horse to follow (in the wild), making the horse lie down, fording rivers, cantering up steep slopes and – even harder – down again, and jumping without saddle and reins are just a few of the diverse schooling exercises that rider and horse went through together.

For both soldier and farmer, therefore, it was vitally important to be able to communicate subtly with the horse and to trust it completely, and it's no coincidence that the horse of all animals was chosen for these tasks:

First, of course, it was chosen for its size and strength, its friendly nature and its desire to do everything right.

Above all, however, it was chosen precisely for its unusual sensitivity, without which such fine understanding would be impossible. Being able to make such a large, strong (flight) animal respond immediately to your thoughts and minimal changes in body tension is unique – and would never be possible with such perfection with an ox, a donkey or even a sturdy zebra.

The widespread belief that prevails today – namely that controlling a horse is synonymous with riding – is therefore a mistake, and this crude "operating" of an extremely sensitive animal (as if it were an inanimate item of sports equipment) has serious consequences for the horse's well-being.

The same extraordinary sensitivity that allows fine communication makes it easy to cause lasting damage to a horse.

And this is exactly what happens with the kind of rough riding that is so widespread today:

Horses suffer physical and mental harm every day because riders confuse "operating and controlling" with riding.

Many of today's riding instructors teach their students under the assumption that crude mechanical control of the horse equals good riding, and of course the students assume that this is right. It is not.

To illustrate this, let's look at two contrasting examples. Both are drawn directly from my own experience, but they happen in similar ways every day in many countries and they have one thing in common:

In neither case is the training horse-friendly.

In both cases the training has no benefit in terms of strengthening, exercising and maintaining the horse's health and in both cases the rider's communication with the horse does not work.

Example I:

An indoor riding arena. Cold neon light shines on the ground, which bears the traces of countless hooves. A rider leads a horse into the arena. The horse is bandaged and gleaming with glossy spray, tiny rhinestones glitter on the browband of his bridle, the noseband cinched tight over puffy skin is in a shiny black patent leather – matching the riders' squeaky clean boots adorned with sparkling long spurs, also studded with rhinestones. The spotless breeches with silicone grip are the same colour as the horse's saddle numnah, bandages and rug, and the rider's matching jacket tops the outfit off perfectly.

In one hand she holds her mobile, on which she is talking loudly, obviously sounding off at someone. With her other hand – in which she also holds the reins – she gesticulates wildly and angrily to add emphasis to her words, oblivious to how this keeps tugging at the horse's mouth and how he keeps recoiling to protect himself and his head from his rider's frenzied, furious gestures.

She leads the horse to a mounting block and jerks the reins hard and impatiently when he doesn't come to an immediate standstill. Still talking on the phone, she mounts and rides around the track in walk. Gesticulating, she speaks loudly and excitedly into the phone and then laughs at something the other person has said, only to revert to her annoyed tone soon after.

From time to time, she absent-mindedly spurs the horse on to go faster.

After five minutes she finishes her phone call, dashes off a few more WhatsApps and, clicking on a last emoji (smiley face with tongue sticking out), tugs violently and persistently on snaffle and curb bit to bring the horse to a standstill at the rail.

Still fixated on her phone, she reaches for the rug with her other hand and drapes it over the rail, revealing the horse's shiny, clipped coat. The two rectangles at spur level on either side of his belly that were spared give an idea of what his winter coat would look like.

Sighing, the rider puts her phone away in her jacket pocket and now hangs her jacket over the gate as well.

Then she takes up both reins, drawing the horse's nose down to his chest, while speaking to him for the first time. "Here we go then," she says and starts trotting. The horse's movements are elaborate; the rider drives him on with every step.

Each time they pass the mirror, the rider gives the reins several sharp tugs, alternating left and right. Not because the horse changed his posture, simply because she is riding past the mirror. A reflex action, as if it's linked somehow.

In this way she trots circles, full track and serpentines, then repeats the whole thing in canter, ending with flying changes and half-passes, sinking her spurs a little deeper into the furry rectangles. Events are only interrupted by a brief stop at the rail when the rider retrieves her phone from her jacket to see if she's had any replies. She taps in a LOL smiley, shortens the reins again, and starts trotting again.

After half an hour of trotting and cantering, she comes back into walk then halt, throws the rug over the horse, puts on her jacket and immediately busies herself with her phone again. Finally, she dismounts and leads the horse to the arena door, where she clamps the phone between ear and shoulder while giving the horse's hooves a cursory picking.

The horse lifts his feet voluntarily, with several long shakes of his neck and head, chewing frantically on the bits to release all the tension and stress that has built up during this "training" session.

Fig. VI: Example image: rhinestones on the ear veil are no substitute for good riding. Force and improper use of the curb are used to exercise "control", but not communicate.

Fig. VII: Example image: pulling in front, stabbing behind: rider signals that the horse can't understand are triggers of stress.

Example II:

An outdoor arena. The deep sandy floor is strewn with pool noodles, poles and tarpaulins. A rider leads in her horse, which is noticeably on the small side for her height. The horse is tacked up with a western saddle and a thin rope halter made of nylon cord, with a thicker rope attached to the underside by a carabiner. The rider uses it to lead the horse through the foam noodles, talking to it constantly.

"No, not that way, through here. Well done! Great job, big guy!"

Then she leads the horse in tight turns over the poles without noticing how the horse stumbles over them because it can't see anything in front of him at such close range.

In the centre of the arena she stops, picks up a long whip from the ground and extends it towards the horse, continually waving her outstretched arm. The horse shies away.

"No, don't walk around me, sideways you dummy!" shouts the rider, waving the whip even more frantically.

The horse doesn't understand what the rider wants from him. He gives a few yawns, a few quick nods of the head, and flaps his lip to relieve the stress that is slowly building up in him, while walking a few tight circles around her to avoid the whip.

The rider maintains a constant flow of words and praise, changes the whip to her other hand and now waves it in the other direction. "Sideways over the poles, just like that. Goooooood jooooob!"

The horse walks between the poles (not sideways over them, as the rider apparently wanted) and walks two more circles around her. "See, this is going great already! Great job, big guy!"

She pats and praises her horse at length, then buckles the thick rope to one side of the thin nylon cord that forms the noseband and a second rope to the other side and leads the horse to a mounting block, from which she heaves her relatively large body onto the relatively small horse with a movement that does not point to an abundance of physical fitness. Once on board, she pats and praises the horse effusively again and rides off.

They shuffle in walk through the deep sand, over the poles and through the pool noodles. Finally the rider asks for trot, kicking the horse's belly with both legs at the same time and giving him a small slap with the whip.

The little horse struggles through the sand with its head stretched out and its back hollowed in the flattest possible trot.

After half an hour (mainly walk, a little trot) the rider dismounts, praises her horse effusively again and then leads him to the tethering post, where he stands motionless with a long straight neck, as if everything is hurting.

There's no need to tie him to it, as he doesn't move another metre of his own accord.

Fig. VIII: Example image: hollowed back, heavy rider, damage to the horse is inevitable – albeit unintended

Fig. IX: Example image: whip combined with painful action of the rope halter – conflicting signals are triggers of stress for the horse

The rider begins to pick out his hooves with her arms stretched out, because she stands as far away from the horse as possible. When the horse raises a hind leg slightly higher while giving a hoof, she immediately lets go of the hoof, jumps back and hits the horse on the croup.

"I told you not to kick!" she shrills. She doesn't pick up the second hind hoof at all, but gives the horse a dish of apples instead. By now the horse has given up trying to understand what is going on with his rider and starts eating the apples – which aggravate his already chronic gastritis.

Two different situations, two different riders, two different horses, two similarities:
The rider's interaction with the horse was unclear and confusing for the horse.
Both riders caused their horses harm, though I'm sure they didn't mean to.

The first rider put her horse in a situation of heightened tension and stress from the outset, giving him an impression of imminent danger. Just by the angry phone call and wild gesticulating while jerking on his mouth.
The horse can't tell whether someone is talking into a phone; it only registers the mood and tone of voice. In this case, both were unfriendly and therefore threatening to the horse.

Horses can sense moods (and especially signs of tension) in other creatures, which enables them to be ready for flight as quickly as possible – so a rider acting like this basically alerts the horse to a threat and puts it under tension and stress. The painful jerks on the mouth, which seemed to the horse not to be related to anything, reinforced its perception that it was in danger.

In this example, the horse's interaction with the rider was limited to obeying and performing; the communication consisted essentially of unsubtle use of bit and spurs. The very fact that the rider has left the coat unshorn at spur level is a clear indication of spur use that is not reconcilable with classical riding.

The constant stabs to his belly, neck pulled down to his chest, tightly buckled noseband and resulting shortness of breath and extreme tension in his head, neck and back all added to the horse's stress. Not to mention the blockages in the hyoid bone, poll, cervical spine, shoulder and withers that the rider has already ridden into the horse with just one "training" session. The excessive head shaking and frantic bit chewing after riding in this case was the horse's attempt to release the tension created by this extreme forced posture.

This horse certainly doesn't associate riding with anything positive, but with pain and coercion. It has become resigned and no longer resists because it has learned that resisting will only cause it more pain. So it just tries to get through the "work".

If you asked the rider why she treats and rides her

horse like this, she'd say she has six horses to ride every day and no time to mess around with each of them for hours on end, it's all about training the exercises after all and that's exactly what she did.

If you asked the horse what it wanted, it would probably say: "A rider who is kind to me. I haven't done anything to her, but she's always yelling at me, she's rough and hurts me – I'd respond much better to kindness (light aids) and also cooperate more willingly..."

And really, shouldn't everyone be able to relate to that? If someone is unkind to you, yells at you, or even causes you pain, do you really want to talk to them? How do you feel when someone treats you roughly? Do you get scared? Or do you get angry and fight back? If it's your boss or colleague who's always yelling at you like that, do you enjoy going to work? Would you call such a person a friend? Hardly.
This is what I meant when I wrote that friendship with the horse is the first basic prerequisite. Because you don't treat a friend unkindly, you don't yell at them, and you certainly don't cause them pain.

The other rider was a complete mystery to her horse. He clearly didn't understand at any point what she wanted from him and wasn't even given a chance to understand. The conflicting signals, constant talking and permanent praise, whatever the horse did, and the punishment for doing something the rider wanted (lifting a hoof), were understandably deeply unsettling for the horse.

It couldn't judge when it was doing something right and when it wasn't, and when it thought it had understood its rider's signal correctly and lifted its hoof, it was both punished for it and then immediately rewarded with a dish of apples.

It doesn't get much more confusing.

The rider was also too big and too heavy for the horse – which is especially worth mentioning because she didn't exercise and ride the horse in a way that would have built up its muscles to enable it to carry the rider without sustaining injury. This horse too is more likely to remember the training as something unpleasant, rather than a lot of fun.

If you asked the second rider why she doesn't get herself a good riding instructor to train herself and her horse healthily and happily, she'd say she doesn't need that. After all, she only rides for fun and doesn't demand a great deal from her horse.

Well, that may be so, but she's still harming it.

If you asked the horse what it wanted, it would probably say: "Clear communication. I don't know what she wants from me, I try my best to do everything right, but I just don't know what that might be... I really thought I had understood the hoof-giving-thing correctly and then she hits me again. And I wish I had more muscles to carry the rider without having backache all the time. Or, if it's not too much to ask – maybe a smaller/lighter rider right away? She's really big and heavy and I have to keep counter-balancing her to avoid falling over..."

Everyone should be able to relate to this too.
Staying with the example of the boss, imagine you have a boss who gives you a thousand jobs to do – without telling you what each job actually is. Who praises you one minute for something you did that you thought might be the job, and the next minute yells at you and throws a coffee cup at you – even though you were absolutely sure you had understood and done the task correctly this time.

How would you like to work under this boss? And how long would you last? Two days? A week? In the hope he'll be able to express himself more clearly?

No wonder this horse also developed stomach ulcers.
And then, to make matters worse, he was rewarded with the worst possible treat for stomach ache (apples), so his "reward" made his stomach ache worse and was therefore a punishment at the same time – no matter how nicely the owner had meant it.

(Which, by the way, also underscores once again why "leisure horses" that "don't have to perform" and are kept in open stables suffer from human-inflicted diseases and pain just as often as "sport horses".)

You can quit if you have a boss like that. But the horses have no choice. They can't just look for another job. They can't even yelp or cry out, at least giving voice to their pain. They can only try to communicate and to make themselves understood. And sometimes they do this in such desperate ways that it can break your heart.

Precisely this is the enormous responsibility that every rider and owner bears and that so many seem simply to refuse to acknowledge:
It is the duty of every rider and owner to acquire the horse knowledge and basic skills that will enable them to handle, keep and ride their horse in a way that will at least do it no harm or injustice.

Chapter 3

Riding should therefore mean fine communication and cooperation with the horse, not its subjugation or domination. The use of the term "riding" for other activities, such as riding a bike or motorcycle, has unfortunately reinforced this widespread misunderstanding of the horse as a machine that comes with an instruction manual.

So here is **the very first basic rule**:

Riding is an art that, if it is not to harm the horse, can only take place in harmony and (voluntary) cooperation with a highly sensitive living creature.

The first prerequisite for good riding is therefore, unsurprisingly, the need to acquire comprehensive knowledge of the nature, body and characteristics of the horse.
Riding also demands the highest level of body control and concentration from the rider, as the horse perceives and responds to every change, no matter how small, that the rider may consider unimportant.

Riding is an art that is immediately detrimental to the horse if the rider lacks the necessary knowledge, body control and fitness or has failed to learn or understand the basic rules and techniques required for this cooperation.

Which brings us to the **second basic rule**:

It's always the rider who makes the mistakes. The horse only responds to what the rider thinks, feels or does.

To ensure success, therefore, I believe it's crucial to give riders images they can really relate to.
In this book you won't read things like:
"Get your horse on the bit and ride a volte".
Because that's what I'd call an "empty instruction".
A phrase with no explanation, that doesn't help the rider at all and, if the rider hasn't yet learned what is important, makes even the best exercise pointless or even detrimental.
These empty instructions, commands such as:
"Grip with your knees!", "Heels down!" or "Head lower!", are unfortunately sometimes counter-productive to teaching real riding.
Partly because even in their basic principles they don't regard riding as the fine art it should be – they are really just an instruction manual. But also because they don't teach riders what they actually want to do with their horse – and how best to achieve it.

"Head lower" is of no help to the rider, it contains no real clarification, no explanation of how to do it, it's not even clear what it means.
It's simply an instruction.
And specifically, it's one of those instructions that

usually end in a posture that is harmful for the horse and is achieved by the rider simply pulling on the reins and the horse lowering its head to avoid the painful pressure of the bit on the tongue, lower jaw bone and gums.

This is not art, it's force and mechanics. Riding, however, is not about forcing a horse into a posture.
It's about being so skilful that the horse adopts the desired posture of its own accord. (Which, by the way, to stick with our example, has nothing to do with getting the "head lower", which many instructors and riders think is "contact" or "forward-downward".)

The same applies to other empty instructions. A command like "Grip with your knees!" will only lead to a tense seat and the rider straining to grip and hold. Which in turn is enough to stop the horse from being supple and responsive.
Horses respond to cramping and tension (provided they're not already completely jaded) with cramping and tension.
It's as simple as that.

So an instruction would be better worded like this:
"Wrap your thighs round the horse – turn your knee inwards a little and allow the leg to lie loose", and already the following prerequisites for a smooth seat with fine and precise influence are in place:

- the knee makes contact without gripping
- the hip stays mobile
- the leg lies loosely and smoothly on the flank
- the foot points forward
- the heel can bounce with the movement

It is vital to be able to imagine what you want to do and how your body and the horse should feel. For that, you need explanations that are clear and understandable.

Just as important as the above is to have a detailed plan in mind of what you want to practise on that particular day in that particular training session, and then be able to change that plan instantly if it turns out that the horse would rather canter another lap in forward seat, or maybe even that you'd be better to do a long hack that day.

The exercises in this book can also help with this, because they can be used to quickly and easily design a fixed but flexible training plan tailored to the form of both horse and rider on that particular day.

You and your horse won't learn very much or may even have a negative experience if you trot lap after lap on a circle without instruction from a competent trainer and without any focus, doggedly trying to "get your horse on the bit".
Your horse will start to fidget and resist, or simply

shuffle mechanically through the sand – but in neither scenario do you refine your coordination and cooperation with the horse. Which is not to say that riding a circle is a pointless exercise, quite the opposite: it is actually very helpful. But if you just do lap after lap around the arena, it has little to no positive effect. On the other hand, horse and rider both learn a lot if you spend the same quarter of an hour riding something as apparently simple as careful transitions between walk and trot:

you will work on your concentration, refine your aids enormously (if you do it right) and notice that your horse is suddenly no longer afraid of the dangerous corner, pays attention and suddenly goes on the bit all by himself. (More on this starting with Exercise I.)

For the exercises to achieve their effect, the following minimum rules also are essential:

The third basic rule:

However trivial and tedious a task may seem, riders should approach it with the same seriousness and enthusiasm they would apply to more demanding tasks, giving absolute priority to accuracy and detail. Otherwise, the effect is immediately lost or even reversed.

Being able to ride flying changes isn't enough to make you a good rider. Good riding develops from the seemingly boring little things.

The fourth basic rule:

The horse's nostrils should be the foremost point of the animal at all times. Not the forehead, and certainly not the ears. Only with an open poll can the horse's musculoskeletal system work optimally and without sustaining injury. How high the horse's head is carried depends on what we want to work on. Our goal is essentially to obtain two postures: a stretching of the horse's neck forwards and downwards, i.e. nose level with the point of shoulder and below, through to nose on the ground – but always with the nostrils in front; and self carriage of the horse.

This means that the horse raises its withers, carries its neck and head higher (the nostrils are still the foremost point), lowers its croup and shifts its centre of gravity backwards.

The fifth basic rule:

You should never hold on tight to the reins. If you're not getting anywhere with a horse, you should immediately lay the reins on its neck and take a break, or even call it a day. This means: Depending on the mood and the nature of the miscommunication, dismount immediately or walk out of the arena on a long rein, praise the horse, put him back in his box or turn him back out to pasture, then start again the next day – and *work smarter this time.*

Because as we saw under rule two, it's not the horse's fault if the rider asks for something he doesn't understand or isn't capable of performing.

It's the rider's responsibility to make sure at all times that they train and work with the horse in such a way that he can do what is asked of him.

Many of the mistakes made today at the expense of horse health could be avoided by following this short set of rules.

It is certainly not easy to engage with this correct way of riding and to change as a rider if you've only ever learned to control your horse by exerting force and "cracking down".

And it's especially hard if you've already had a lot of negative experiences and are possibly even afraid of riding.

So I'd like to offer some advice at this point:

first, if you've read this book and want to try things differently – take a different approach, pretend it's your first day with the horse.

Even the welcome may be friendlier (from the horse's point of view), as you may perceive and see your horse differently as a result of what you've read here.

When grooming, saddling and bridling your horse, you will probably pay more attention to whether it is showing signs of pain or discomfort; you may want to use a soft bit or not use one at all and buckle the noseband (if you haven't done so before) according to the two-finger rule. You'll probably already have had the saddle fitted (to your horse, not your comfort) by a competent saddler, in short: you're ready to work differently with your friend.

Second, on the extraordinarily important subject of the fear that many riders have, I'd like to say a bit more:
If you're afraid of handling or riding a horse, find an experienced trainer to help you get rid of these fears as quickly as possible. And if that doesn't work:
maybe riding isn't for you.

If you're anxious or uncertain, things can get really dangerous really fast around a horse. Not because the horse is wicked, but because it takes your tension and anxiety as a sign of imminent danger.
And of course riding is more dangerous than other activities, and of course a horse can kill a person. At any time and with ease. If it wanted to, a horse could put anyone in hospital or into the afterlife without much effort; a single well-aimed kick would be quite enough.
But they don't do it, or if they do it's only because they see no other option, can't escape, are poorly treated or severely overworked. And even then, it's rarely a targeted kick. When treated correctly, horses are among the gentlest and friendliest creatures on earth and are vastly superior to humans, not only in strength but also in temperament.

No horse would deliberately hurt a person – unless it couldn't be avoided or the horse had been previously mistreated.

Horses that could finish their riders off with a well-aimed bite or kick instead suffer day after day due to those very riders' fear and incompetence.
Due to pain and measures inflicted for fear of losing control, due to sharp bridles, hitting and Rollkur/LDR – and yet they don't snap a hair on their riders' heads, though they could easily do so. Simply because it is not in the gentle nature of the horse.
Maybe all riders should think long and hard about this.

Riding isn't tennis, where you don't care how you hold or handle the racket or even if you slam it to the ground in frustration and simply replace the broken one with a new one. In riding, living creatures suffer due to the false ambition of countless riders, and their failure to realise that riding may just not be right for them.

So a few pointers:

Anyone who wants to ride should be clear about the following:

- Falling off is part of it, no matter how well you ride. You absolutely will get hurt as a rider. And sometimes even seriously.

- Bolting, spooking and shying are normal horse behaviour and can only be averted by the rider's skill and confidence and the horse's trust in its rider.

- Learning to ride is only possible with hard work, discipline and patience.

- Riding means first and foremost taking full responsibility for the horse and always putting its welfare first.

- Riding means communication, partnership and trust. It has nothing to do with control, subjugation or even violence.

Please don't try to learn to ride if you're actually afraid of it.

In other situations in life, such "confrontation therapy" might make sense and be helpful in overcoming fears – but here, it happens at the expense of another living being, and that's just not acceptable.

Note: you put your horse under tension due to your own anxiety or uncertainty, and convey a sense of imminent danger. Unless you have an especially confident horse, it's only a matter of time before he'll decide to run. Or fight.

And why that's the case is what we'll look at now.

Chapter 4

Before turning to the individual exercises, we should talk about the horse's flight instinct. Because something that sounds so innocuous is crucial to the success or failure of our work with the horse.

Just as much now as it was a thousand years ago, the fight or flight instinct is ingrained into every horse to ensure its survival.

Its content is fairly simple:

If danger threatens, run away as fast as you can. If you can't escape, fight until you break free or until you die.

This is an automatic process that, once set in motion, is very difficult to stop. The horse can't decide to return to normal now, to calm its heartrate and relax its muscles. This doesn't happen until the horse is completely sure it's no longer in danger.

However, it's important to know that the horse's flight instinct can also be triggered and maintained by pain: a horse that's in pain due to a sharp bit in its mouth, an uncomfortable saddle or a heavy rider on its back, or a leg or stomach problem, won't be supple and relaxed and will exist in a semi-permanent state of fight or flight – with far-reaching consequences for its health.

In fight or flight mode, not only are its heartrate and muscle tone increased, but large amounts of stress hormones are released into its bloodstream. As in humans, stress predisposes to gastritis and stomach ulcers, often leading to deficiencies due to poor absorption of vitamins and trace elements and, of course, accompanied by severe pain.

The supply of blood, nutrients and oxygen to the heart and muscles is increased and the supply to organs deemed "unimportant" for flight or fight, such as the skin or digestive system, is reduced. Recurring digestive disorders and colic are therefore no surprise in stressed horses and are a real cry for help.

The susceptibility to skin and respiratory conditions comes as no surprise either, because the immune system is effectively suppressed in order to put all available energy into flight or fight, which naturally makes the horse vulnerable to any fungal infection or other bug that might be going around.

As if all of this wasn't bad enough, the brain's performance shuts down to reptilian level so the horse doesn't start thinking about which direction to run in, but just runs – not the best precondition for mastering complex tasks.

And finally, as mentioned earlier: the muscles go into a state of high tension and no longer contract and relax alternately, making it impossible to develop muscle strength and size.

These evolutionary biological processes are perfect for a quick escape. But totally unsuitable for working a horse in a way that promotes health, for the following reasons:

1   Continually high muscle tone inhibits muscle growth. Only a muscle that alternates between positive contraction and relaxation can build up and become stronger.

2   The brain shutdown means that our horse can't really absorb or learn anything, and to demand complex performances from him in this state would not only be extremely unfair but entirely pointless.

3   A horse in fight or flight mode isn't listening anyway. These processes are geared to sheer survival; everything else simply pales into insignificance.

So trying to work with a horse under tension, pain, fear or stress is not only pointless, but in most cases causes it further harm.
As riders, therefore, we should prevent this from happening at all costs.

The good news is that, in the vast majority of cases, there are signs that a horse is about to run or explode, and a horse can be trained to be generally braver and more stress-tolerant, so it doesn't reach the threshold for flight so quickly.* (*More on this in *"Equine Sports - on the horse's back"*)

So it's important to know about the fight or flight instinct, and to be able to recognise a horse on the verge of it.

A crucial point here is the adaptation of the horse's senses to the constant flight readiness: the fight or flight instinct is so strong in the horse that several of its senses are specifically geared to perceiving danger.

The horse hears much better than humans and on completely different frequencies; it can see much further, but almost nothing in its immediate vicinity; it has an acute sense of smell and, most importantly for riding:

It can "read" emotions in other living beings.

A horse can perceive the tiniest signs of tension, fear or excitement in the creatures around it.

This includes other horses, dogs, cats, mice, wild animals, birds – or even people.

Simply perceiving such tension gives a horse an instinctive "heads-up" of imminent danger and shifts it automatically into the first stage of the flight or fight instinct.

It can happen as easily as that.

At the same time, it is this extraordinary sensitivity that enables us to guide our horse solely by focusing our thoughts and varying our body tension accordingly.

To illustrate this ability in the horse, I'd like to tell you about an experiment: horses and riders were fitted with straps to measure their heartrates, then the riders were instructed to ride around an arena at one side of which a person was standing with a rolled-up umbrella.

For a few circuits of the track, the heartrates of horses and riders were recorded to establish a baseline: all of the heartrates were calm and within the normal range.

Now the riders were told that the person with the umbrella would open it up with a jerk the next time the horse and rider approached.

In every case, the rider's heartrate soared in anticipation of the shock this would cause to their horse.

And here comes the remarkable part:

The horses' heartrates rose in parallel with those of their riders, without the horses knowing that the umbrella would be opened on the next pass and indeed without it being opened at all.

For the horses, absolutely nothing had changed; they simply responded to the increased tension of the people on their backs.

For me, this experiment illustrates very impressively the extent of truth there is in the old adage that every rider will have heard at some point:

"Horses can sense fear in a rider."

This statement is much more than just a typical riding instructor's comment; in fact, it's vitally important.

The basic rule for all riders is: stay calm and relaxed even in difficult situations and under no circumstances allow yourself to be infected by your horse's nervousness or anxiety.
Never lose your self-control, be calm and consistent at all times, and don't punish your horse or cause him pain.
It's crucially important for a flight animal to remember every bad experience, to ensure its survival, so the horse does precisely that.
A single situation like this can destroy months of hard work.

So at this point I'd like to remind you of basic rule number 5 and add:

Don't ride with coercion, pressure and pain; all of these factors also increase the horse's stress. Riding in "Rollkur/LDR" or other forced postures (as well as any other type of violent, rough riding) entails far more negative consequences for the horse than just the pain and resulting blockages in the mouth, jaw, poll, neck, withers, shoulder and back.
We want to achieve precisely the opposite with our riding: we want to strengthen and empower the

horse to prevent it from becoming damaged – physically and psychologically.
And we can only succeed in this if a) we have gained the horse's trust, and b) our training involves no danger, pain or fear for the horse.

Riding with ease also helps to improve the situation for the horse in this context. A rider whose communication is fine and precise has a calming and confidence-inspiring effect on the horse, it happily follows the signals and is not so quick to panic.

I assume this is also why all the horses that used to bolt with me or buck me off and spook at every blade of grass would suddenly, with my grandmother in the saddle, develop a laid-back, sunny disposition and give a loose, swinging canter on a long rein at the perfect pace.
And this underscores what many people before me have said in similar ways:
You just need to know how to ride and understand the horse, then (almost) everything else becomes superfluous.

Something else that's very important for our fine riding is this: as a herd animal on the plains, with nowhere to hide, horses developed a style of communication that is as quiet as possible, to avoid attracting the attention of predators. Horses perceive loud noises as frightening and pay attention to every facial expression, every gesture, every tilt of the head or ear, every leg position. This is one reason why it is so easy to teach horses all sorts of tricks in "free schooling", and it's also one reason why so many horses switch off as soon as their riders are around.

A rider who talks to his horse constantly, gestures widely or is simply just loud represents an imposition for the horse. It develops almost a "noisy brain syndrome" – the rider just sends far too many signals all at once. This is why calm, self-contained and competent riders who know what they are doing are so well-liked by horses.

So be aware that your horse not only reads your emotions, but also your facial expressions – and that it might read something into a hand gesture that you didn't mean to convey.

This is precisely what I mean when I say we have to find a common language. A misread cue is a misunderstanding, and if the horse suddenly does something the rider didn't want, then that too is nothing more – or indeed less – than a misunderstanding.

Chapter 5

Before we start the exercises in the next chapter, let's take a brief look at the structures in the horse's body that are most important for us in this context as riders.

This is especially relevant to riders because, as we saw earlier, we cause most of the harm to our horses by exerting too much influence on the horse's "head".

I think it helps to understand how far-reaching the consequences of making the horse submit head-down in a "frozen pose" are, if you at least know the following connections:

1. Hyoid bone and shoulder/forehand

We can block a horse's hyoid bone within seconds by using hard hand action, sharp bits or coercive measures such as riding in Rollkur/LDR, but also by "sawing" or by unconsciously using strong rein aids when riding with a bit.

The horse's hyoid bone is a bony structure comprised of several articulated joints. It hangs like a swing from the horse's temporal bones between the branches of the lower jaw.

The front part of this structure (or "apparatus") forms an extension that stabilises and moves with the tongue, while the rear part connects to the larynx among other things.

If the hyoid bone cannot move both up and down and forwards and backwards at the point where it connects to the skull, and move freely to and fro with the tongue, or if the mobility in both joints is disrupted, this also restricts the mobility of the larynx and uvula among other things, impeding the act of swallowing.

In extreme cases, horses may be reluctant to drink and have trouble eating, and drooling is often seen in horses with a fixed or blocked hyoid.

However, a blocked hyoid bone can not only stop the horse from eating and drinking properly, it can also cause restricted movement and forehand lameness.

One of the muscles that pulls the tongue backwards for swallowing is the omohyoid or "shoulder hyoid muscle".

This originates under the shoulder blade in the shoulder fascia and attaches to the hyoid process of the hyoid bone.

This means that there is a direct connection between the hyoid apparatus and the horse's shoulder. If this muscle is over-tensed, as in horses ridden in Rollkur/LDR, with tight nosebands or with other types of coercion, the tongue stays permanently pulled backwards.

Which naturally restricts first the mobility of the tongue itself and second, in a direct way, the mobility of the shoulder.

If these muscles are under permanently increased tension, the shoulder starts to hurt.

– A common sign of soreness in the forehand (other than resistance to having the shoulder groomed) is a lack of "go".

Many horses that are labelled as "lazy" or "sluggish" actually have pain in their shoulders or forehand.

The horse has no bony or joint connection attaching its front legs to its body.

The shoulder and humerus are attached to the body by muscles, ligaments and tissues alone, which basically allows for better shock absorption and more flexible movement.

But as soon as these shoulder muscles become tense, sore or overloaded, this immediately affects the horse's overall action.

A lack of "go" is just one sign among many. By the time the horse shows any lameness, it has usually sustained significant harm, has compensation in the back, neck and pelvis, and needs comprehensive treatment to restore its physical well-being.

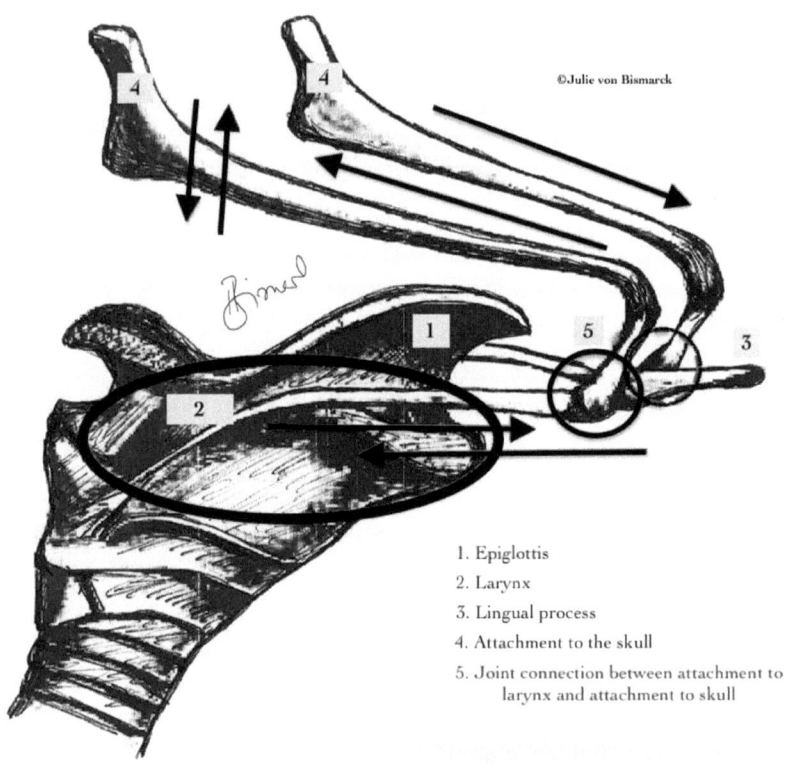

©Julie von Bismarck

1. Epiglottis
2. Larynx
3. Lingual process
4. Attachment to the skull
5. Joint connection between attachment to
   larynx and attachment to skull

Fig. X: The hyoid bone of the horse

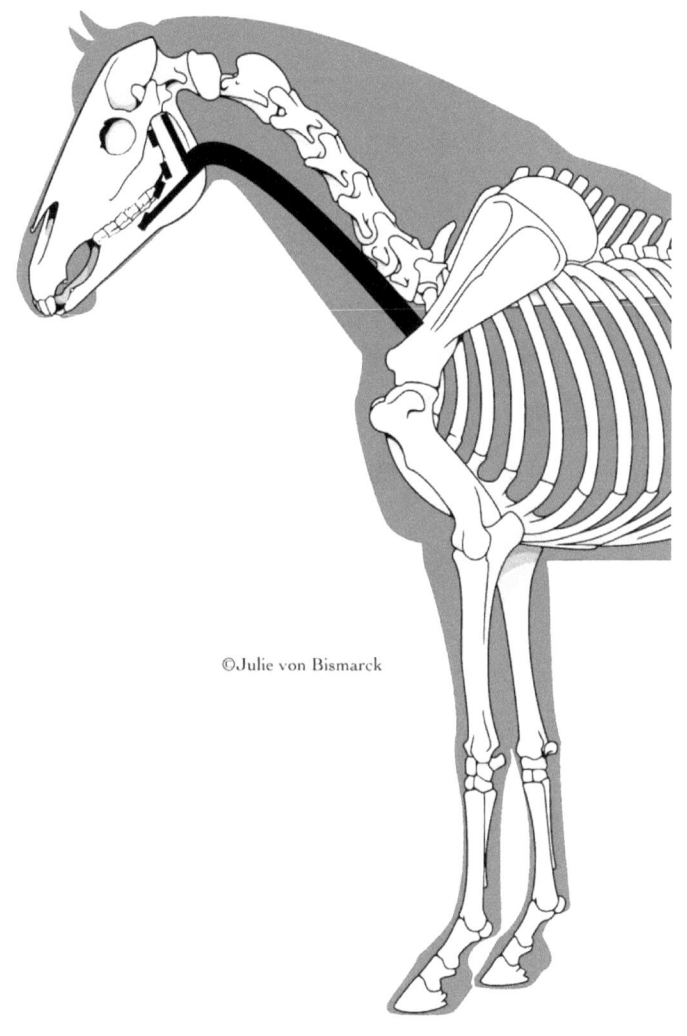

©Julie von Bismarck

Fig. XI: The shoulder hyoid muscle

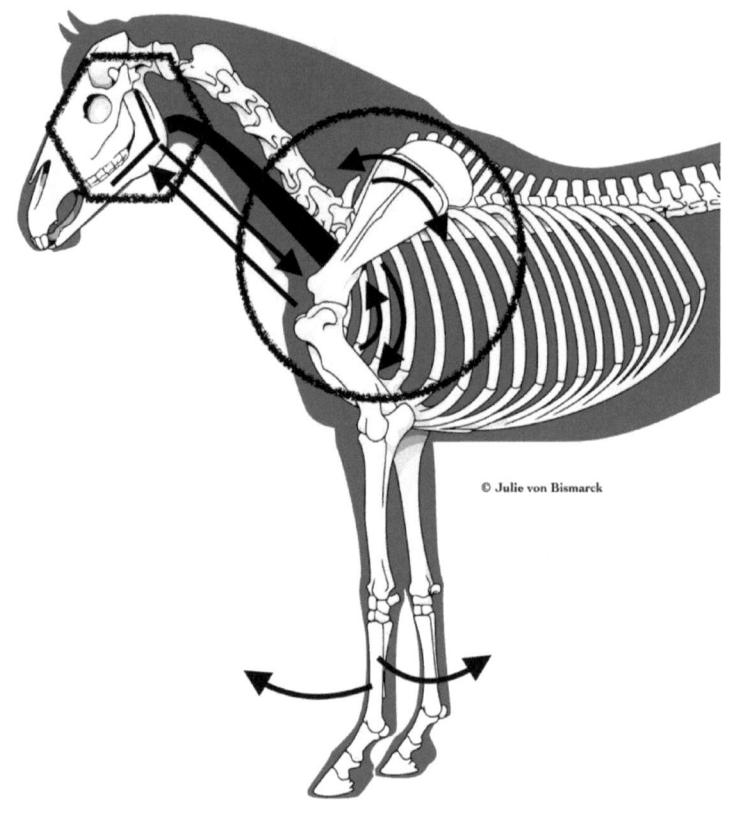

Fig. XII: The hyoid bone and the movement of the forehand

When the horse brings its leg forward, its shoulder blade slides backwards/down on the thorax and the angle in the shoulder joint, i.e. between shoulder blade and humerus, opens.
When the horse brings its leg back, i.e. in the support phase, the shoulder blade slides forwards/up and the angle in the shoulder joint closes.

If this mobility, this sliding of the shoulder blade on the thorax, is restricted by the tension in the shoulder fascia, this has the following consequences:

1 The horse can no longer bring the affected leg forward as far as the "healthy" leg, so it loses reach.
2 In the supporting leg phase, when the weight is on the affected leg, the inhibited forward slide of the shoulder blade causes a painful tension in the muscle groups connecting the front leg to the horse's trunk. This tension extends into the neck and upper back.

You can think of it as an extreme tension in the shoulder and neck area. In the worst case, you may get numbness in your fingers, headaches and back pain, and become unable to turn your head or move your arms freely without pain.

A horse that seems "sluggish", doesn't extend its forelegs very far forward or won't bend or cross its forelegs may have pain in this shoulder and neck area.

So it's very important to ride horses in such a way as to loosen the shoulder/neck area, preventing tension here. This demands fine contact and careful use of the rein aids (when riding on the bit).

2. Temporomandibular joint and sacroiliac joint

The horse's temporomandibular joints are another structure that riders can easily damage or lock through poor riding or clumsy handling.

As with the hyoid bone, the damage in this case is not limited to the joints – on the contrary, a hard hand also affects the mobility of the hindquarters. More precisely, it affects the transmission of thrust from the hind legs via the pelvis to the back.

The temporomandibular joint (TMJ) connects the lower jaw and the temporal bone of the skull. It combines a hinging and a sliding action to allow different movements:

- Forwards and backwards
- Right and left
- Rotating/grinding

This mobility is crucial for the horse, not only for chewing, but also for movement.

A blockage of one TMJ tends to extend quickly to the other one too, as the lower jaw (mandible) is fused in the centre below the lower incisors, so its two branches cannot be moved separately.
If they do move separately, the horse should immediately be taken to a veterinary clinic, as this is very likely to mean a broken jaw.

Horses in the wild rarely get a blocked jaw, but if they do it's to compensate for a blockage of the sacroiliac joints or due to a dental condition, whereas TMJ blockages are a common finding in riding and carriage horses.

The long lever of the mandibular branches and the position of the bit are assumed to play a decisive role in such blockages:

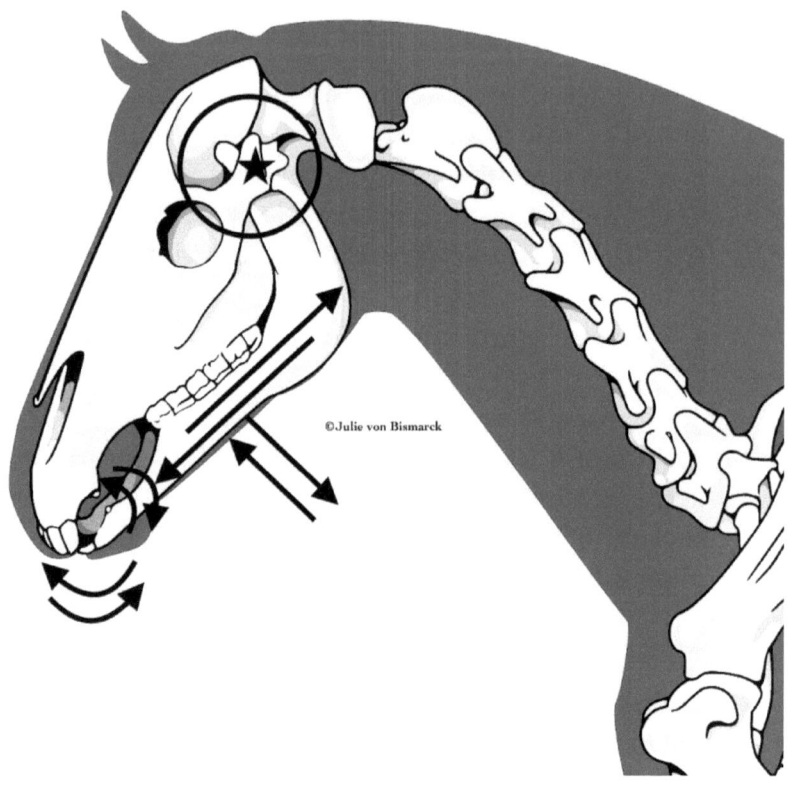

Fig. XIII: The temporomandibular joint and its directions of movement

A downward pull or pressure on the front third of the lower jaw, i.e. the site where not only bits, but also chiffneys (anti-rearing bits), lead-ropes, etc. are attached, causes the long mandibular branch to act like a lever, multiplying the forces acting on it many times over.

This means that the TMJ is put under a pressure it is not designed for. This pressure is absorbed by the muscles, which tense up accordingly and then remain tensed, restricting the mobility of the joint: the TMJ becomes blocked.

A hard hand, forced over-flexion, or a rope pulled through the mouth because the horse won't enter the trailer, can cause a permanent blockage of the TMJ within seconds.

Not to mention the other health consequences.

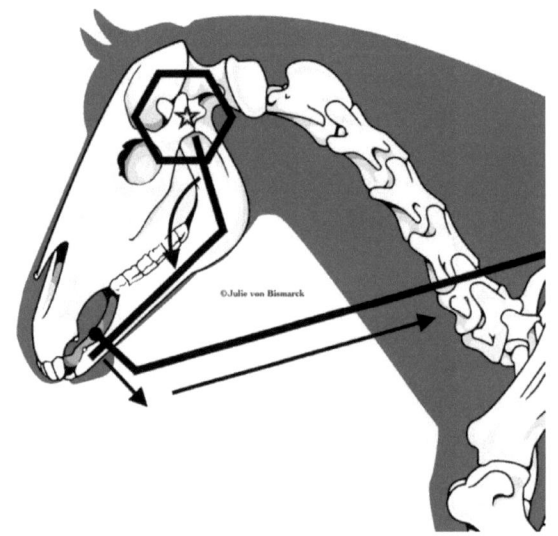

Fig. XIV: Lever action on the long mandibular branch puts pressure on the angle of the jaw. As the jaw cannot open here (the bone is continuous), this pressure extends to the TMJ itself. The joint is not designed to take this type of stress, so the surrounding muscles come to the rescue by tensing up, locking the joint (= TMJ blockage).

A blockage like this means that the TMJs can only move to a limited extent – with serious consequences for the horse:

1. Pushing the lower jaw forward:

This is an automatic movement in which the lower jaw slides forward as the horse lowers its head.
This movement is geared towards optimising feed intake: the incisors are arranged one on top of the other in order to tear up grass and plants, and at the same time the sliding forward of the lower jaw creates space in the TMJ itself for the grinding movements that are then needed to crush the food.

2. Grinding and lateral movements:

Like many herbivores, the horse chews with a grinding or circular motion, rotating the lower jaw. This crushes the feed between the broad molars, almost like grinding between two millstones.
At the same time, this unique chewing motion mechanically expels saliva from the salivary glands. This is especially important for the horse, as saliva acts as a natural buffer to neutralise its stomach acid. And since a horse's stomach contains acid all the time, not just when it eats, this buffer is extremely important to stop the acid attacking the stomach lining.

The lateral movements of the lower jaw to right and left are not just part of chewing; they are also crucial for every turn the horse makes.
This is because it is the lower jaw that initiates any change in the horse's direction of travel, by shifting slightly in the intended direction.

3. Pushing the lower jaw back:

This movement occurs as the horse raises its head. It virtually "closes" the TMJ, making chewing difficult in this position.
The pushing back of the lower jaw brings tension into the horse's neck and back, which extends into the hindquarters.
In short: when the horse pushes its lower jaw backwards, this movement automatically produces a tense, upright position.
Remember the chapter on the fight or flight instinct: lifting the head not only widens the field of vision, but also brings tension to the hindquarters (the horse's "engine"), to allow an effective, immediate escape from the situation.
In riding, we turn this to our advantage when we ride a horse in an upright, elevated position.

This shows again how ingeniously all of the horse's movements are coordinated, no matter how small, and how important they are.

As these movements are very similar in humans,

this gives us an excellent opportunity to see for ourselves what a restriction of these relatively small but crucial movements can mean for a horse.

Try it out; the results are remarkable.

Exercise 1:

Stand up straight but relaxed and soften your jaw slightly: when the jaw is in neutral position, the upper and lower teeth don't meet – the same is true for the horse.

Now move your head, chin first, slowly forward-downward without changing anything else.

Notice how your lower jaw slides forward with the movement. Close your eyes to feel this sensation better.

Stand up straight again and this time tightly clench your teeth. Now repeat the same movement.

Notice how much tension builds up, extending right down through your neck, and how the movement may even become painful.

The movement is still possible, but it is no longer loose, natural, effortless and flowing.

The same is true for a horse if its lower jaw is prevented from sliding forward.

Exercise 2:

Stand up straight but relaxed again, soften your jaw and walk forwards normally, turning to the left after a few steps.

Notice how your head initiates the movement and your shoulder and upper spine follow.

But now focus consciously on your lower jaw and notice how it shifts in the intended direction first, even if only slightly, before your head, shoulders and spine then follow.

Now try the same thing again, this time turning to the right; interestingly, the movement is usually "easier" on one side.

Now clench your teeth again and repeat the experiment. Notice again how pressure develops throughout your head and how unnatural or mechanical the movement suddenly feels.

Remember this the next time you buckle your noseband or flash strap, as it will definitely encourage you to follow the two-finger rule. Always leave two adult finger-widths between the nose bone and the noseband or strap.

Exercise 3:

Stand up straight but relaxed, soften your jaw and now consciously pull your lower jaw backwards towards the back of your head.

Notice how this movement automatically pulls your head back and puts your neck and upper back under tension = you stand up straight and your body tenses.

Now try exaggerating the movement: pull your lower jaw as far towards the back of your head as possible; the chin automatically goes to the chest and the neck tenses, extending into the upper spine.

This is the position a horse is put in when in Rollkur, LDR or any tight posture.

Notice how your throat closes up, breathing becomes harder and it takes an effort to swallow.

Now try to chew in this position. Notice how limited the movements are and how much tension you need in your lower neck muscles to perform them at all.

I'd be amazed if you can hold this extreme position for more than half a minute.

My neck muscles start to hurt within seconds.

This shows how a horse must feel when its nose is pulled down to its chest.

And it shows why we should make sure that movement in the horse's TMJs is possible and pain-free at all times, in order to train the horse without harming it. By the way, this also includes regular check-ups by a specialised equine dentist.

The importance of this becomes even clearer if we know that the TMJs' connections extend into the pelvis, because:

Limited mobility in a TMJ leads sooner or later to a blockage of the sacroiliac joint on the other side

of the body, and vice versa.
This means that a blocked TMJ can not only trigger the problems described above, but also paralyse the entire pelvis and the transmission of thrust and impulsion from the hindquarters to the back.

Let's take a look at the biomechanics:
The sacroiliac joints are the only connection between the pelvis, i.e. the hindquarters, and the horse's back. They are not true joints, but a connection consisting of taut ligaments, tissues and muscles between the underside of the iliac crest and the sacrum. Due to the enormous forces that act and are transmitted here, the range of motion in the sacroiliac joints is very small, benefiting stability.

Mobility in the sacroiliac joints, i.e. a tiny but measurable spring-like motion of the iliac blades in the connections to the sacrum (one right, one left) formed by ligaments and muscles, is therefore of crucial importance, as it is here that thrust is transmitted from the hindquarters to the spine.

It can be imagined like this:
The weight-bearing hind leg pushes off and the resulting impulsion/thrust reaches the pelvic ring via the hip joint.
The ilium compresses forwards and down with the movement at the sacrum, the last part of the horse's spine before the tail vertebrae = when the hind leg pushes off, backwards and out,

transferring the thrust/impulsion from the ilium/pelvic ring to the sacrum and from there to the lumbar spine. In the lead phase and when the foot takes off, the ilium springs backwards/upwards in the sacroiliac joint.

It's like a wave that originates with the hind hoof pushing off from the ground and from there spreads via the knee and hip and is then transferred via the iliac crest to the sacrum, from where it continues via the lumbar and thoracic spine, the cervical spine and poll/TMJs, finally arriving at the horse's mouth.

Some of you may have learned to ride under the old guidelines, and if so you'll know the rule that you can only collect impulsion with the hand if you've first generated it in the hindquarters.

The old riding masters may not have known about the connection between TMJ and pelvis, but they were perfectly aware that the rider's hand, i.e. the action of the rein on the bit/lower jaw, can override the horse's hindquarters and interrupt the wave-like motion of thrust flowing through its body.

When riding, always remember how poorly designed the horse's TMJ is to cope with pressure, so how quickly you can cause these problems with the action of your hand.

Remember the jaw movement exercises too: these movements may be small but they are absolutely essential for natural, relaxed movement that benefits the horse.

Only this ensures that the right muscles are used and prevents strain, pain and wear and tear in the horse.

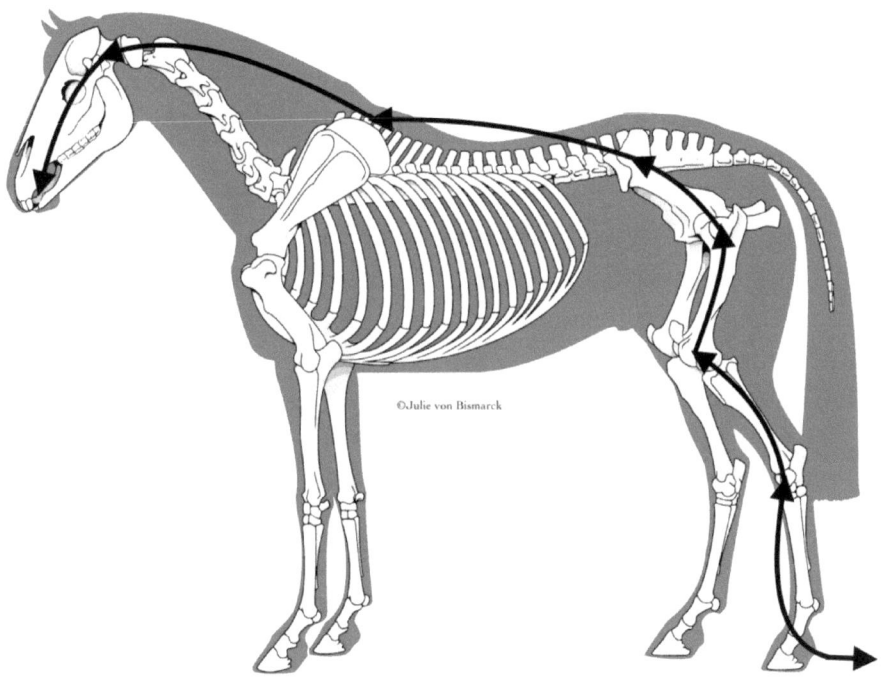

Fig. XV: The wave

3. The poll

The poll is another structure that we can quickly damage when riding or handling the horse.

Heavy pressure on this area, whether from rope halters, unsuitable snaffles or riding in a tight neck position, leads to tension, pain and restricted movement.

The pain can be so severe that the horse suddenly becomes "head shy", refuses to be bridled or haltered, rears as soon as the rider applies pressure, shakes his head, shies more and becomes more jumpy.

Remember: these reactions are not a sudden attack of viciousness on the horse's part, but an expression of pain.

When most people hear the word "poll", they probably think first of the connection between the skull (occipital bone) and the first cervical vertebra (atlas), but it also includes the connection between the atlas and the second cervical vertebra (axis).

Part of this second cervical vertebra extends into the first, and the term "poll fracture" often means a fracture of this piece of bone or "process".

Because the poll is not a single joint, this structure in the horse is often referred to as the "upper cervical joints" or "head joints".

The movements that should be possible in the poll are:

nodding movements between the first cervical vertebra and the occipital bone, or "yes joint", and rotating movements between the second cervical vertebra and the first cervical vertebra, or "no joint".

The junction between the first and second cervical vertebrae is the only place where "flexion" can take place in the horse, and only if the first cervical vertebra can move freely and is not blocked in one direction.

A horse with a blockage or pain in the poll will be hard to flex, and will tilt its head and have problems in contact.
If you misinterpret this and use force and auxiliary reins to compel the horse to adopt the desired posture, this can cause it significant harm.

One reason why riding with an "open" poll is so important is that mobility in the head joints should not be impaired.
Riding a horse tightly puts considerable pressure on the first and second cervical vertebrae, leading to tension, pain and relieving postures.
So always make sure your horse has an open poll when riding.

The term "open poll" is often misunderstood, so let's put it another way:

The horse's nostrils should be the foremost point of the horse at all times; this is when you have an open poll.

In the vertical direction, the nostrils are only slightly further forward, but they are still the foremost point of the horse.

By watching out for this, you're already taking a huge step towards horse-friendly training.

Training in the field is important, but so is feeling the actual movements of the horse, training the concentration of rider and horse and developing precise riding for targeted exercising of the horse.

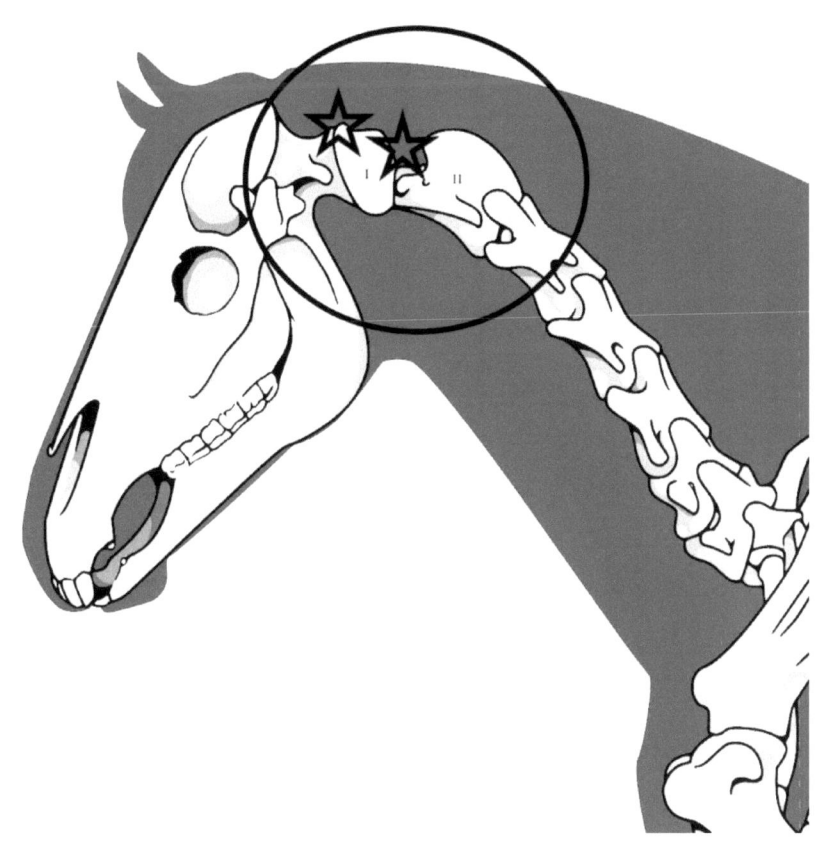

Fig. XVI: The poll of the horse

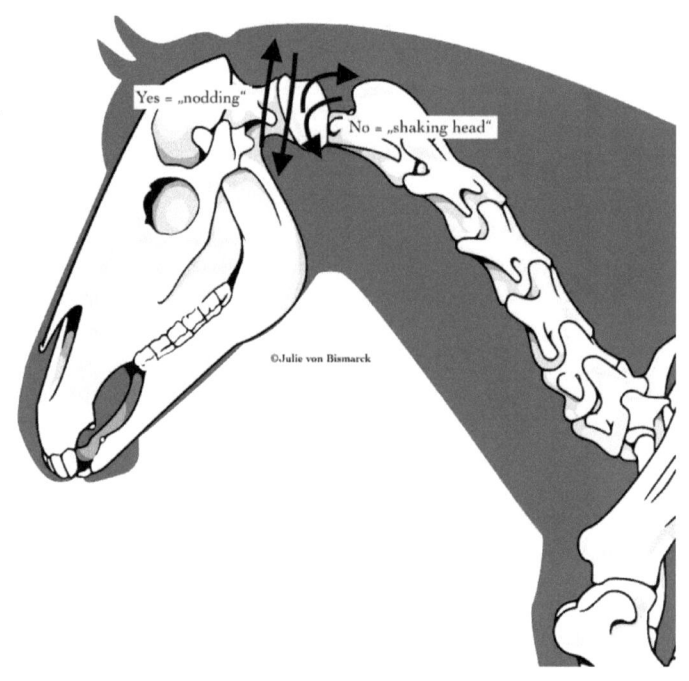

Fig. XVII: "Yes" and "No" joint

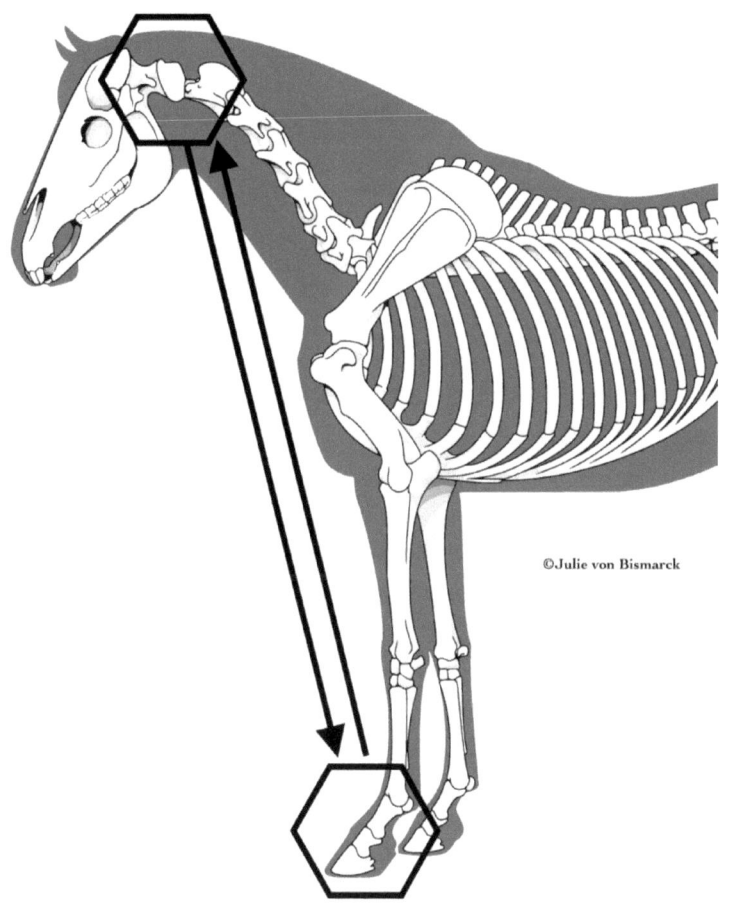

Fig. XVIII: Connection between poll and hooves, fetlock head

Chapter 6

Now let's move on to the practical exercises that will help to refine our communication with our horses.

Requirements for the rider: sound basic training and a balanced seat (though you will of course continue to work on this every day), an ability to concentrate and physical fitness.

Requirements for the horse: health.

All exercises listed here are suitable for any healthy horse, and – as unlikely as it might seem at first in some cases – any healthy horse can eventually perform these exercises perfectly with focused, regular work.

I know that some people may have doubts, especially when riding a horse that already seems completely jaded due to poor riding or painful handling and has to have every step of trot "dragged out of it", or goes to the other extreme and seems impossible to keep under control without constant rein action.

You'll be amazed how much a horse can change when its training and handling are changed.

There's no doubt that a horse that has been schooled from day one according to classical riding principles, with time, patience and common sense, will find it easier to perform the exercises than a horse that has been "ridden" for a decade solely with draw-reins, sharp bits, tight bridles, coercion and pressure. But even the latter horse can achieve the goal – and that's the wonderful thing about these exercises.

As much as I usually prefer riding in open country, I suggest you practice the exercises first in an indoor or outdoor arena. You need to be extremely focused during these exercises, especially at the start, and that's where boundaries help. So you're not constantly thinking "do I need to steer or brake?" – but also simply for orientation.

When reading the exercise descriptions and before each ride, try to imagine the sequence of movements and your own body tension that each exercise will require. You'll find these "dry runs" enormously helpful when it comes to putting everything into practice: the brain stores the imagined sequences, making sure that your body already reacts while you're thinking.

And this is exactly what your horse will respond to. In other words, your horse will make its movements larger or smaller, or change the gait or direction of travel, as soon as you even think of the task at hand – because you'll intuitively adopt a slightly different body tension and posture. And this is enough for your horse to react.

Lavish praise on your horse as soon as it does something right. Take your time over this and don't stress just because you think you need to complete the exercise.

Praise and positive reinforcement are the key pillars on our way to fine communication with the horse, so they are just as important as the exercises themselves.

Note: Praise is part of training – not an interruption.

As I've already explained, the exercises listed here are all about the little things.
Especially at the start of your new training regime, this includes taking pains to ensure that you sit and give aids correctly and that your horse actually does what you want it to do and doesn't "cheat".
Friendly determination, focus, concentration and consistency are our keywords here.

The exercises can be incorporated into your usual arena schooling. Start with Exercise I and only add a new exercise when you and your horse have truly mastered the previous one. (The only exception is the last exercise, which you can ride whenever you like.)
If you have nothing else to practise, there's no harm in repeating all the exercises you've done so far in the schooling session. But this should be the exception rather than the rule, as it demands enormous concentration from rider and horse.

Either way, take a break after each exercise and walk on a loose rein for 5–7 minutes. You and the horse both need time to process what you have learned.

Stop as soon as an exercise has worked to your satisfaction. It's entirely understandable, but a big mistake, to want to try it again (and again and again) – just because it finally feels good.

Don't do this: you'll most likely come out of the session feeling miserable because the tables usually turn and nothing works any more. We should always aim to stop on a high note, a good feeling, so we can start the next time with that same good feeling.

So end the training after a successful exercise, lavish praise on your horse, canter a bit more or simply call it a day – depending on how much work you have already done.

It pays off to refrain from repetition – that way you can look forward to the next session even more.

Remember that the horse is not a machine and has good and bad days just like any other living creature. If you notice, on a day when your horse is due for dressage training, that it would be better served by a long hack, a gentle walk, or a cross-country gallop, postpone your plans accordingly.

It is absolutely critical to try to make our work with the horse positive all round. I have already explained the negative effects that stress has on the horse's health. If we're aiming for a true partnership with the horse, we need to be as responsive to his sensitivities as we are to our own. By the way, it's also important to change our work with the horse when it's not the horse but the rider who's having a bad day.

After a long day at work where everyone has got on your nerves and nothing's gone right, there is absolutely no point in getting on the horse in a bad mood and with a short fuse and aiming to ride exercises that require total concentration.

As we've already seen, the brain shuts down under stress and can no longer satisfactorily perform complex tasks – this applies of course not only to the horse, but also to the rider.

So if it's one of these high-stress days, your ability to concentrate is not at its best. And since the exercises don't work without a highly focused rider, it's very likely that nothing will work today.

In such situations, many riders soon succumb to frustration – they're already fed up and now "the riding isn't working either"... These riders run the risk of taking their frustration out on the horse.

Don't risk it:

A single case of holding on tight to the reins, a single unfair act because you're fed up, can destroy weeks of work and the trust and understanding built up between you and your horse.

Always remember what we talked about in the section on the fight or flight instinct: horses remember every good experience, and every bad one as well. This is why horses respond so well to positive reinforcement during training, but it's also why a single bad experience is enough to destroy all of our hard-won trust and fine communication.

By riding these exercises and changing our inner attitude as we do so, we are aiming to achieve a feeling that can be described, in very simplified terms, roughly like this:

It feels as if our body merges with that of the horse; every movement the horse makes is transmitted to us and every tiny change in our posture or tension immediately triggers a response in the horse.
You'll understand what I mean when you experience this for yourself for the first time. Then you'll also understand why any form of rough treatment, coercion, pain or sharp equipment has no place in this style of riding.

If this succeeds, you'll soon notice how much more pleasure you get out of riding, how much stronger and friendlier the relationship with your horse becomes – and how much easier it is for you and your horse to master everything.
How much braver you both become in open country, how your horse suddenly responds to your thought-aids and how much better your body control and your horse's posture become.

Once again, the following points are key:

o Praise your horse immediately for everything it does right. Ignore unwanted behaviour.

o Be consistent and ride each exercise accurately down to the smallest detail. Only by being consistent and taking pains over every little thing from the start can you find your way to finer communication later on.

o Never punish. Horses, like all living creatures, learn best through positive reinforcement. Punishment only leads to resistance and a negative association with the experience, never to a lasting learning outcome with positive associations.

o Don't expect miracles. Not even if your horse seems to change immediately in some exercises: only practice makes perfect – and not only you, but also your horse has good and bad days.

o Don't be surprised if you're sore in muscles you didn't know you had.

o And above all, don't give up! A proper riding education takes many years and riders continue to learn throughout their lives.

Tips for riding the exercises:

• Ride the exercises without spurs (this is a must!) and only on a normal snaffle or without a bit (in this case please use a normal bridle/noseband, no levers, no knotted/rope halters, no other equipment with a sharp action). Any kind of "aids" such as sharp bits, bitless bridles with lever action, knotted/rope halters, curb bits or auxiliary reins defeat the purpose of the exercises and you won't achieve the desired effect. The point of these exercises is to learn to trust each other, to "rely on each other", to communicate with each other with subtle aids and to have a friendly conversation.

If the rider brings weapons to this conversation – and yes, even a bitless bridle or halter counts as a weapon if it has a sharp action – this approach is futile:

1   Riders rely on these extra aids and are under the impression that they cannot ride their horse without them. But that's exactly what we want to change. We want to gain the feeling of being able to achieve exactly what we want with our horse – with just ourselves, our thoughts and our "conversations" conducted through muscle tension and movements. When this succeeds for the first time, your connection to the horse deepens all by itself – and with it, your relationship. And this in turn is the

basis for good riding.

2 Because – no matter how good the rider is – you can't rule out the possibility that the action of these aids may inflict pain or coercion on the horse during training. Both would destroy trust rather than building it, put the horse under tension and leave it with a negative association.

- Make sure you get yourself lunged regularly for seat exercises, so you can develop a loose, relaxed seat on the horse, on both reins.

- Wherever the rider doesn't need increased body tension, try to sit like a "rag doll": in other words, as loose and relaxed as possible.
We want a horse that is supple and responsive – and that only works with a relaxed rider.

- Start off gently on your "better" side, i.e. the side on which tasks are easier for you and your horse.

- Always perform each exercise in exactly the same way on both reins. So if you have practised it twice around to the left, repeat it twice around to the right.

- Don't try to improve your "worse" rein by riding it more often – especially if there's no experienced trainer there to correct and help from the ground: rather than improving, you risk reinforcing the mistakes you're already making. There are often several reasons for a worse rein, and correcting them takes an overview that you don't have from your position on top of the horse. Instead, continue to ride all of the exercises evenly on both reins and try to take the good feeling from the easier rein over to the harder one. In the vast majority of cases, this works pretty well.

- Use voice aids until the fine coordination works. Just be sure to use them as precisely as you use all of your other aids. If you talk constantly to the horse, it will switch off. As we saw in the chapter on the fight or flight instinct, horses communicate with each other as quietly as possible, minimising sounds, so as not to attract the attention of predators. Constant exposure to sound is therefore likely to be extremely disturbing for a horse.

- If it's much easier to perform an exercise on one rein than on the other, this may point to pain, blockages or restrictions of movement. In such a case, get yourself and your horse checked by an experienced osteopath or physiotherapist and rule out any faults in the equipment.

- The goal is to be able to ride all of the exercises without using the reins. When this succeeds, the reins can be taken up again because the rider has learned to control the horse so well by other means that the reins play only an accompanying and fine-tuning role – and are no longer considered the rider's "main tool".

Fig. IX: An example of positive tension without pressure – this is how (with slightly higher or lower head and neck) we want to ride our horses in the following exercises.

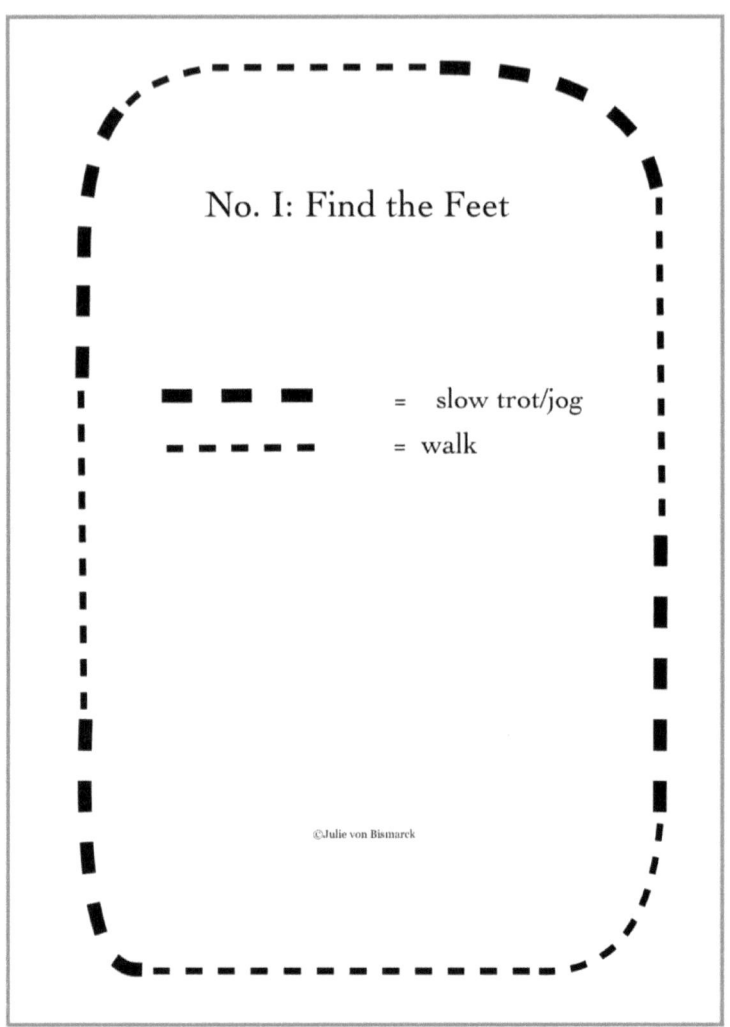

No. I: Find the Feet

▬ ▬ ▬ = slow trot/jog

▬ ▬ ▬ ▬ ▬ = walk

©Julie von Bismarck

Exercise I: Find the Feet

My first exercise sounds simple but you'll soon discover that it's not simple at all.

I call this exercise "Find the Feet" because it's designed in part to give the rider an accurate feel for each of the horse's four feet – a vitally important step on the road to fine riding. This exercise also promotes submission and suppleness in the horse, as well as responsiveness.

It goes like this:
Go large around the track.
Ride 10 steps in walk, then 5–6 slow steps in trot, then back to walk. Concentrate on each movement of the horse and change down to walk or trot on at the precise spot that you have marked in your mind.
If it's working well already, you can try to keep precisely to the 10 steps in walk and 5 steps in trot.

The rein length shouldn't change during this exercise and the contact should be very light. You'll notice that you have to start thinking about the transition one or two steps in advance, in order to hit the mark.

Crucially, both changing down to walk and trotting on should be done without using the reins. To come down into walk, pin your "ears back" and think about walking, use your voice too if you like.

To trot on, think about a very slow trot, don't push your horse.

Make it trot on slowly, and I mean really slowly, because you'll want to transition back down into walk right away. You'll soon notice that your horse is responding to your thoughts as they form and how easy riding feels all of a sudden.

Ride the exercise for up to ten minutes in total (stop early if you get a few good transitions in a row!), repeating it the same number of times on each rein.

The vast majority of horses soon figure out what it's all about and start trotting or walking on their own – so count the walk and trot steps carefully, vary the numbers during the session and be meticulous about using your aids.

As simple as it sounds, it takes a little practice to get it right. But don't be discouraged, because once you and your horse can do this exercise, you'll have taken a giant leap forwards towards fine riding and a healthy horse.

Having "control" of the horse's four legs without using the reins is a vital accomplishment for any rider, if only because it avoids a lot of accidental influence on the horse's jaw and tongue, which can help to prevent many blockages in this area.

Once the exercise is working really well, you can try it on the inner track, serpentines and circles – and of course in the great outdoors.

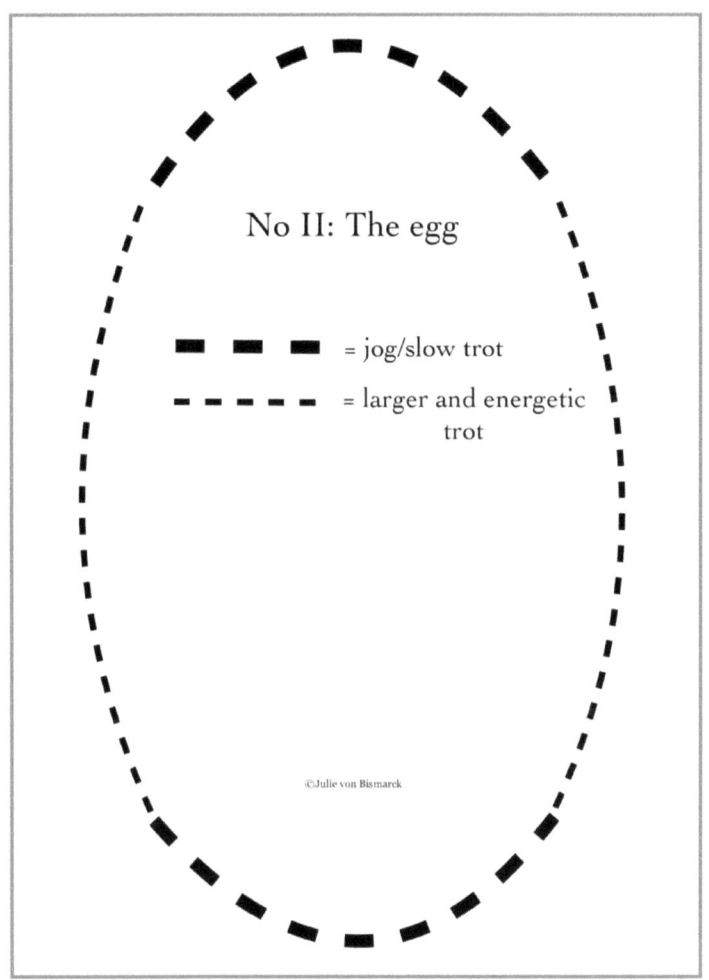

No II: The egg

▬ ▬ ▬ = jog/slow trot

▬ ▬ ▬ = larger and energetic trot

©Julie von Bismarck

Exercise II: The Egg

The aim of the exercise is to get the horse stepping up and coming down in response to the rider's finest leg and weight aids, and to achieve a relaxed swing through the body.
As you progress, you should be able to ride the transitions without using the reins and the difference between the two trots should become as wide as possible.

Like the first exercise, this one is also ideal for warming up. Ride in rising trot on a large oval or egg shape, aiming to expand your horse's movements on the long sides and bring him back to a smaller, very slow trot on the short sides.
The important thing in this exercise is to ride and feel every single trot step very carefully – it's not a case of "long side, step on the gas, short side, throttle back".
To lengthen the steps on the long sides, think of your horse's movements as becoming larger, not getting faster. Imagine the back is coming up to meet you, the horse is lifting its belly and the trotting steps are covering more ground as a result.
To reproduce this image, wrap your legs around the horse's belly, aiming to lift it up to make room for the hind legs to reach further forwards underneath.

Note that the larger you want the movement to be, the more the belly needs to be out of the way – because it's only the larger movements of the hind legs that make the horse's whole action realistically larger.

In reality, of course, it's more about the back arching and working freely, but as an image, "pulling up the belly" is extremely useful.

Initially, therefore, your driving aids will come from heavier or lighter application of both legs and increased positive tension in your body; later, the change in your horse's action will be triggered just by the change in your body tension at the thought of a "larger or smaller trot".

Be careful not to "stand up" actively in rising trot, but to really let yourself go with the horse's movement.

Your stomach should be tensed (which, by the way, means always sticking your belly button out while riding) and your legs should "give" and not grip the horse too tightly.

As you're riding on a curve, it's also very important to focus on limiting the horse's outside shoulder with your outside knee/thigh and using your outside lower leg to stop the horse's hindquarters from falling out.

In Exercise I you learned how it should feel when the horse is on a straight line – now you can take this feeling with you to a curved line. Even on a curve, the hind legs should step naturally into the front leg's tracks – and not land inside or outside them.

As with every exercise in this book, it's all about paying attention to the little things: you basically drive with both legs, but you need to be able to change the type of pressure, tension and position in each leg separately and at any time in order to respond immediately to aspects of the horse's movement.

You want to get your horse performing trot steps of a certain size – bigger on the long sides, smaller on the short sides – and if possible you don't want to use the reins. This means you may need to grip more tightly with your thighs mid-movement and straighten up more in order to make the horse's movements smaller again, or you may need to take off the knee/thigh pressure and instead slightly increase the tension in the lower leg to allow the horse to trot larger again.

Or you may have to push on with the inside leg and simultaneously with the outside leg, but only for one stride with the latter, and then immediately bring it into a guarding position from which you can still encourage the horse's outside hind leg to keep it going forward.

Don't worry: what sounds so complicated is actually quite simple. Once you have developed a feeling for this way of giving aids and these movements, you will automatically do it right.

To bring the horse back into a slow trot on the short side, remember to pin your ears back again and think about trotting very, very slowly – as in Exercise I.

As you do this, imagine the horse's large, ground-covering movements becoming smaller.

To picture this in your mind, it helps to think in terms of bigger and smaller, rather than faster and slower. In the end, it's the size of the movement that changes the speed.

Make sure your horse stays straight in the transition and doesn't "cheat", for example by swerving with the hindquarters, and also watch out that he doesn't "dive" but the nostrils stay in front.

After a few smaller, more sedate trot steps, give up your "holding-back" body tension again, allowing your horse the freedom to expand its movements again.

Ride the exercise for up to five circuits on each rein and then practise something else. At the end of the session you can come back to this exercise and ride two repeats (one circuit on each rein), giving the reins.

This exercise should be ridden in a real forward-downward position at first; later, it can also be done in an upright, elevated position and developed into an extended trot alternating with passage or even into piaffe.

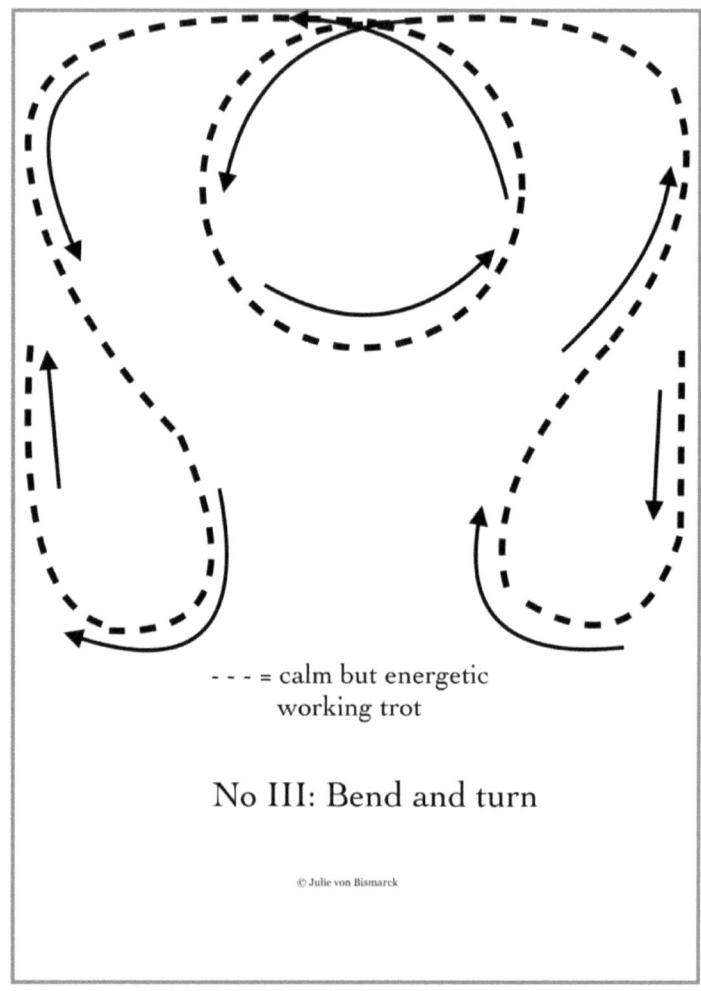

- - - = calm but energetic
working trot

No III: Bend and turn

© Julie von Bismarck

Exercise III: Bending and Turning

This exercise helps to supple the horse and encourages responsiveness (including that of the rider) as the rider needs to initiate the new flexion and bend very carefully in the changes of direction. Repeating the same patterns over and over also helps the horse and rider to concentrate fully on the movement sequences and the tasks at hand.

It goes like this:
Go large around the track in a steady but active working trot. In general I would recommend rising trot, but if the horse is prone to rushing or the rider lacks confidence, it can also be done in sitting trot. In the middle of the long side, ride a demi volte (half circle and back to the track, or "teardrop"); in the middle of the short side, ride a volte (circle and back to the track); in the middle of the long side, ride another demi volte, and so on.
Repeat the exercise up to ten times in total, so that you've ridden five voltes on the right rein and five on the left.
If you and your horse find this task difficult, do a few repeats on each rein and then ride twice around the whole track in a lively canter. Then start the pattern again on the other side of the arena.
Like all of the exercises, you can incorporate this one into your normal training "as you go along" and vary the number of repeats.

How it should feel:

We're aiming to ride the horse into the demi volte with a nice flex and bend, using inside leg and outside knee with a guarding outside calf; the outside lower leg not only prevents the hind leg from falling out, but is already driving on slightly; halfway to the rail, it becomes the bending and driving new inside leg and the old inside leg comes to lie in a guarding position behind the girth.

Many riders simply leave the outside leg in this guarding position during the volte, so here's a little tip: in my experience it can often be useful, especially in voltes, to give a small forward impulse with the outside lower leg as well. In any case, make sure to use the inside and outside lower legs independently in this exercise: i.e. inside leg if you want to move the inside hind leg or achieve more bend: impulse if you want to encourage the inside hind leg to step on more actively; let the leg lie smoothly if you want to bend the horse around it.
And the same with the outside lower leg: impulse if you want to move the outside hind leg; let the leg lie lightly behind the girth if you want a guarding action (and apply more pressure if you want the outside hind leg to step sideways under the horse's body).
As ever, listen to your horse with your body and react only if really necessary.

In this exercise too, try to imagine the route and your body position and stay passive, except for focusing your thoughts. If passive doesn't work, you can always try more insistence.

Make sure your pelvis (hips) and shoulders stay parallel to those of the horse, which means that in the demi volte on the right rein you should first pull your right shoulder back and push your right hip forward, then sit straight for a moment, and then pull your left shoulder back and push your left hip forward.

Look at your horse's shoulder girdle to see if your own shoulders are parallel to it. Then do the same with your pelvis, though you can only feel rather than see this.

On the curved line, the horse's inside hip comes forward further than the outside hip, which should be the case for you too, so you don't block the horse in the bend.

In the turn, try to use your inside leg to encourage the horse's belly to lift, so the belly doesn't prevent the inside hind leg from stepping forward.

Your leg should aim to send the belly up so it's "out of the way". This image is useful for correct use of the leg aid and can also be used in between times for the outside leg.

No IV: The square I

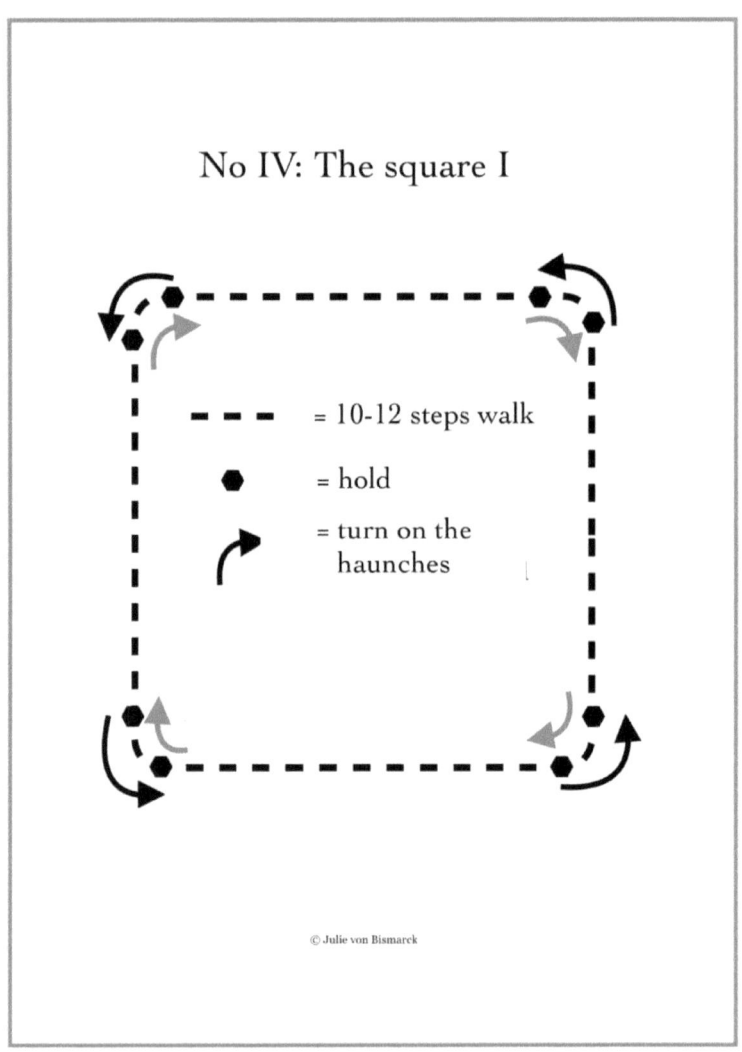

= 10-12 steps walk

= hold

= turn on the haunches

© Julie von Bismarck

Exercise IV: The Square I

This exercise is about turning the horse's shoulders/forehand, a key basic requirement for a straight horse and also one of the most demanding requirements for the rider.

Developing a feel for each of the horse's shoulders and how the rider's body needs to act in order to control them independently is one of the basic principles of fine riding, together with speeding up and slowing down the horse. When you've found out how to point the horse's forehand (and therefore its neck and head) in different directions without using the reins (as you did in Exercises I and II with the transitions between two gaits and within a gait) you are already more or less able to ride entirely without reins.

Which doesn't mean you should do – as a rider it just gives you a new sense of freedom to feel that you hardly need the reins and it is of course a major step in preventing blockages, injury and pain in the horse.

This exercise is primarily about the accuracy of the steps and the concentration of rider and horse, aiming for precise fine coordination and communication. In the final version of the exercise, the pair should keep to the exact number of steps and perform a neat quarter turn on the hindquarters in each corner – and the rider should need no or minimal rein aids. However, to start with in our turn on the hindquarters we do without flexion and bend and leave the neck as straight as possible, riding it a little differently than the classic "turn on the haunches".

Apart from improving the fine coordination between rider and horse, this exercise encourages the horse's hindquarters to take the load and mobilises the forehand, obliging the rider to control the horse's shoulder by seat alone – something that many riders find very difficult.
Most riders try to achieve this by using the reins.

It goes like this: Ride on a square in the centre of the arena, which it's best to mark out with cones. For even better orientation and support, you can start by laying down a slightly larger square of poles, which you then ride on the inside. Many riders find this helpful, especially in the turn on the hindquarters, because it acts as a visual boundary.
Ride 10–12 steps in walk along the first side of your square and stop before the next pole. Count slowly up to ten, insisting that your horse stay perfectly still during this time. Then initiate the turn on the hindquarters by turning the horse's outside shoulder.
The image in your mind at first should be of a horse with a straight neck, as if neck and shoulders were a single unit to be turned without flexion or bend. (You can add both later once this is working well, and if your horse offers it right from the start there is nothing to stop you, but it's easier to work with the "straight neck" at first.)

Ride on, increasing the pressure from your outside thigh and at the same time taking off the inside thigh pressure and applying both calves to make the horse walk on.

Use your outside guarding lower leg to support your outside thigh/knee in turning the horse's outside shoulder, almost by turning the rib cage too. Use your inside lower leg to give further impulses if needed, to make the horse step around smoothly but without rushing.

In your mind's eye, imagine your shoulders staying parallel to those of the horse – so if working with a "straight neck" you should rotate both shoulders as a unit in the direction of travel, twisting from your thoracic spine. Your pelvis stays fairly straight, so you have a rotation in your thoracic spine.

When adding flexion and bend, you would pull your inside shoulder back and push your inside hip forward slightly. Your inside lower leg then takes on more of the task of bending and controlling the inside hind leg, to stop the horse from falling in. Your outside leg also supports this bend, generally lying a little more firmly on the horse.

As this example shows once again: riding means concentrating on tiny little things! The horse responds to the rider's body (and thoughts), so it is solely the rider's responsibility to influence the horse precisely enough that it responds "correctly".

If these aids are not enough at first to get your horse to turn the forehand around the hindquarters, hold a whip at the horse's outside shoulder for support. (Only apply or tap very briefly if necessary, and of course never hit with the whip.) Once your horse understands the task, put the whip back on the wall or fence and keep practising without this support and with the least possible pressure.

Don't make the mistake of trying to pull the horse round on the inside rein or pushing it round with the outside rein.
It is best not to think about the reins at all, but focus solely on your seat.
Imagine that both reins were broken and you had to turn your horse almost on the spot without reins.

Turn the horse by 90 degrees so that it stands with its head pointing in the new direction along the second side of the square. To keep it from turning further, you will need to increase the pressure from your inside knee/thigh and reduce the outside knee/thigh pressure. You will also need to adjust your driving aids and simply allow the lower legs to lie loosely against the horse to achieve a correct halt.
Stop again, this time only for a count of four, then ride on again.
Continue like this until you have completed one

circuit of the square, then change the rein.

You will probably notice that you or your horse find the exercise easier on one rein, but don't be tempted into doing it more often on the worse rein.

Again, as a reminder: be sure to ride all of these exercises evenly on both reins and try to take the good feeling from the easier rein over to the harder one.

Ride the exercise for a maximum of six circuits, i.e. three on each rein.

No V: The square II

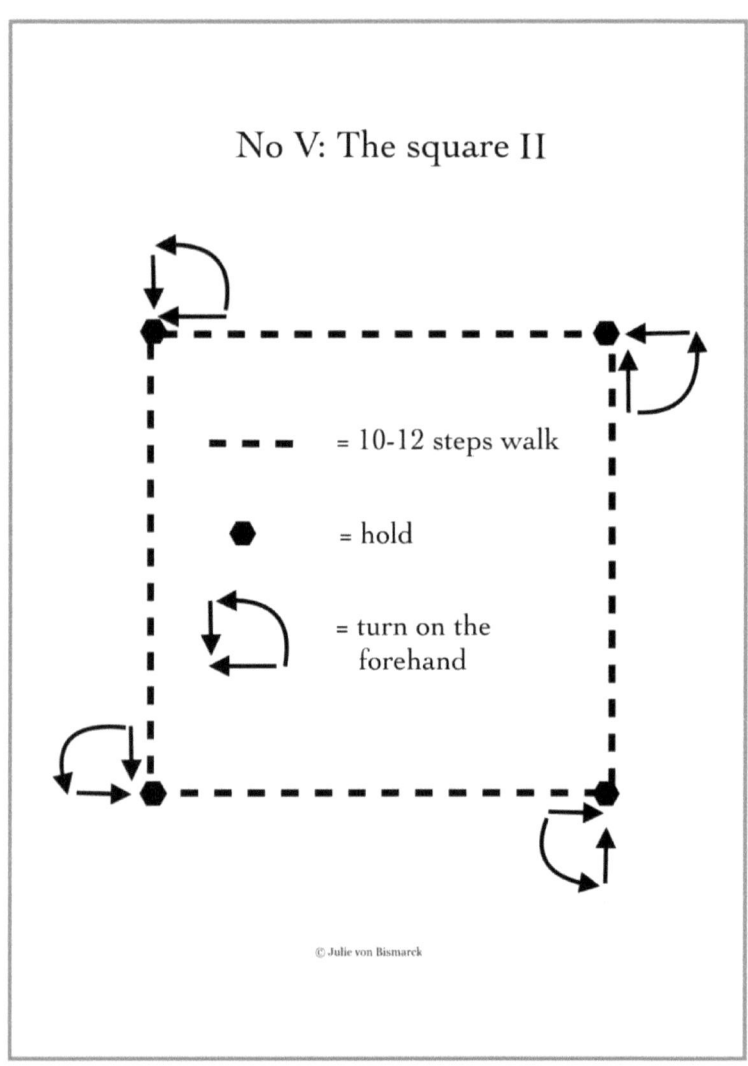

= 10-12 steps walk

= hold

= turn on the forehand

© Julie von Bismarck

Exercise V: The Square II

Like the previous exercise, this one is primarily about the accuracy of the steps and the concentration of rider and horse, aiming for precise fine coordination and communication.

In the final version of the exercise, the pair should keep to the exact number of steps and perform a neat quarter turn on the forehand in each corner. The rider should no longer need rein aids.

This exercise also mobilises the horse's hindquarters, as well as its hip joints, pelvis and sacroiliac joints.

It is also an excellent exercise for curing the horse of "leaning on the bit" and reducing the rider's reliance on rein aids.

If you have already laid poles in a square for support, you should now ride along the outside of the square.

It goes like this: Ride 10–12 steps in walk on your square, as in Exercise III, and halt. Count slowly up to ten again, making sure your horse stands perfectly still. Now ride a quarter turn on the forehand, sitting up straight and thinking of "standing" (as in stopping) while pushing the horse's hindquarters out with your inside lower leg. During this it is important to apply your own outside leg with feeling, and to tense your back more to stop the horse stepping forward. To start with you can use the reins, until you and your horse have found the right coordination.

Usually it doesn't take long until riders are able to perform the turn on the forehand correctly, even without reins. This is when you can take up the reins again, because now you're no longer relying on them but only using them to accompany the actions of your body.

No VI: The square III

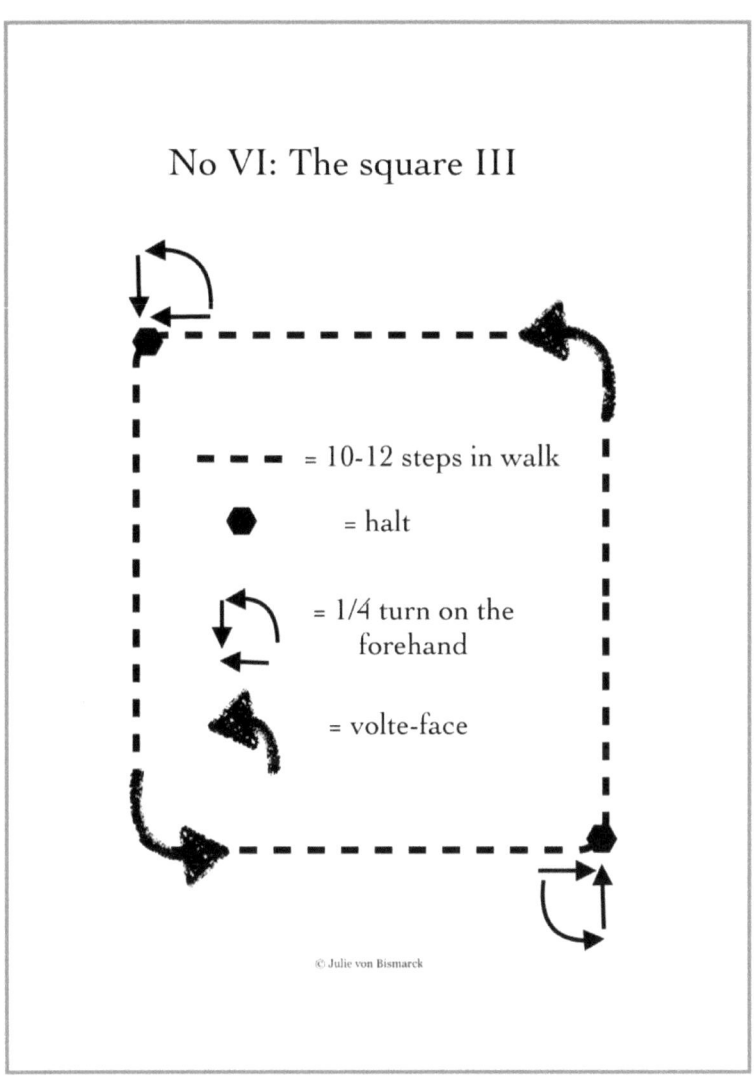

= 10-12 steps in walk

= halt

= 1/4 turn on the
forehand

= volte-face

© Julie von Bismarck

Exercise VI: The Square III

This exercise combines the two previous exercises, with the slight modification that a half pirouette is ridden instead of a quarter turn on the hindquarters.
The transition between halting and turning and the turn in the movement is of special importance here.
The Square III should not be included in the training until horse and rider have mastered Square I and II.
In this exercise, we now combine the accuracy of halting and turning out of the halt with the quarter turn of the forehand around the hindquarters, flowing out of the movement.

The aim of the exercise is to increase the horse's attention, the rider's focus on conscious aid giving and the mobilisation of the horse's forehand and hindquarters. Here too, as you progress, rein aids will become unnecessary at some point.

It goes like this: Ride on the same square again (poles won't work now, but you can put jump stands in the corners), bring your horse to a halt after ten steps in walk, count slowly up to ten, ride a quarter turn on the forehand as described, then make the horse stand again briefly. Now ride on again in walk and after ten steps turn the horse's shoulder/forehand around the hindquarters for the next corner. The hind legs more or less on step the spot, while the forelegs cross and describe a quarter-circle.

For this quarter turn on the forehand, you basically use the same aids as for the turn on the hindquarters, except that you don't want to interrupt the flow of movement.

In other words: you are aiming to integrate the quarter turn of the front legs around the hind legs, which are stepping on the spot, into the movement sequence and ride on in walk immediately afterwards. As far as the next corner, where you halt again and turn on the forehand.

For the half pirouette, think again about aiming to turn the horse's outside shoulder. Here too, it is very important not to try to pull the horse round with the inside rein.

Try to imagine the horse's neck as completely straight at first – you can always add flexion later. It is much easier to turn the shoulder if the horse has a straight neck or even a slight outward flexion.

Around three steps before the half pirouette corner, shift your centre of gravity slightly backwards onto your tailbone, tense your back to get your horse's attention and allow your legs to fall loosely. To initiate the turn, again increase the outside knee/thigh pressure while reducing the inside knee/thigh pressure, take the outside lower leg back into a guarding position and drive forward with a loose inside lower leg.

By adjusting the tension in your back, you can very easily determine the speed: make sure your horse turns smoothly but without rushing it.

I always keep count, as it helps me focus on every step. Depending on how big or small your horse is and his natural reach in the stride, the number of steps will differ. But once you've ridden two quarter turns, you will know that and be able to keep count.

Ride the half pirouette a little "bigger" to start with, rather than holding your horse back too much.

Imagine we are aiming to ride a corner in the smallest space possible, and to do this we turn the horse's outside shoulder around the hindquarters, which are stepping on the spot, while keeping its neck relatively straight.

Keeping the hindquarters moving with our inside leg is very important because this is our "engine" and we want to ride on smoothly immediately after the corner.

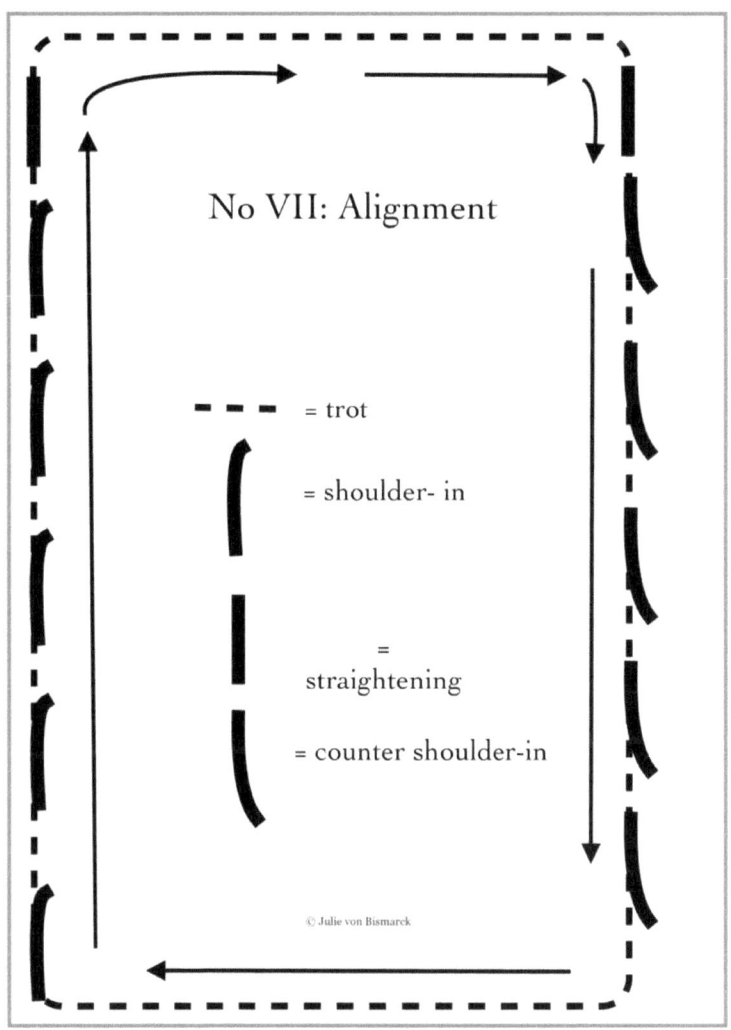

No VII: Alignment

- - - = trot

= shoulder- in

=
straightening

= counter shoulder-in

© Julie von Bismarck

Exercise VII: Alignment

The aim of this exercise is to work on the coordination between rider and horse and to give them both a sense of when horse and rider are actually aligned and straight. All horses have a "hollow" and a "stiff" side, as every rider knows.
But humans too usually have a stronger and a weaker side and are often just as "crooked" in themselves as the horse, without realising it.
So it's not just about working on the horse's natural crookedness, but the rider's as well.

Back in my grandmother's riding lessons, this exercise was a firm favourite for making any horse much straighter in just a few minutes. You'll be amazed how few circuits it takes on each rein to get a much straighter horse and a sensitive seat.

It goes like this:
Ride large around the track in a steady but active rising trot.
Ride deep into the corner and take up flexion from the corner along the long side.
To do this, push the horse's outside shoulder slightly inward with your outside thigh and knee and keep driving on with your inside calf.
Your inside knee lies loosely on the horse without applying pressure, to allow the outside shoulder in.

Watch out that the outside hind leg, controlled by your outside lower leg, doesn't fall out.

Your shoulders should turn again with the horse: think outside shoulder slightly "inward" – which does involve pushing the shoulder forward, but produces a different movement if you imagine moving and aligning your shoulder exactly parallel to that of the horse.

So now do just that, and move both shoulders as a unit, as if you had a coat hanger stuck in your shirt.

Crucially, when your shoulder girdle/coat hanger turns inwards, your pelvis must stay straight. The horse's hindquarters keep going straight, so your pelvis stays straight too – parallel to the horse's pelvis.

Ideally, take up a little less flexion and never flex the horse by more than 30°.

Check whether you can see the inner hind leg between the front feet – if so, it's correct.

If you have a mirror on the short side of the arena, use that; if you don't, ask someone on the ground to look (from the front).

Before reaching the corner on the short side, take off the pressure of the outside thigh/knee, leaving the guarding lower leg as it is, ride deep into the corner again and then turn on the second track before the next corner.

You really need to anticipate here, because this is only a few steps. Once on the second track of the next long side, ride your horse in counter shoulder-in.

This means push the horse's old inside shoulder out with your old inside thigh/knee, guard its old inside hind leg with your same-side lower leg, and drive on with your old inside leg, now the new outside leg.

Your shoulder girdle now turns outwards, parallel to the horse's shoulders, while your pelvis stays straight – because the horse's hindquarters also stay straight on the second track.

Here again, check yourself and the horse in the mirror or ask someone on the ground to take a look. Before the next corner, realign your shoulders and the horse's forehand with its hindquarters, ride back to the track and start over again.

Ride five circuits on each rein, ideally as part of your warm-up. Any time you feel one of you is going crooked again during your session, you can add in another couple of circuits.

No VIII: Sideways

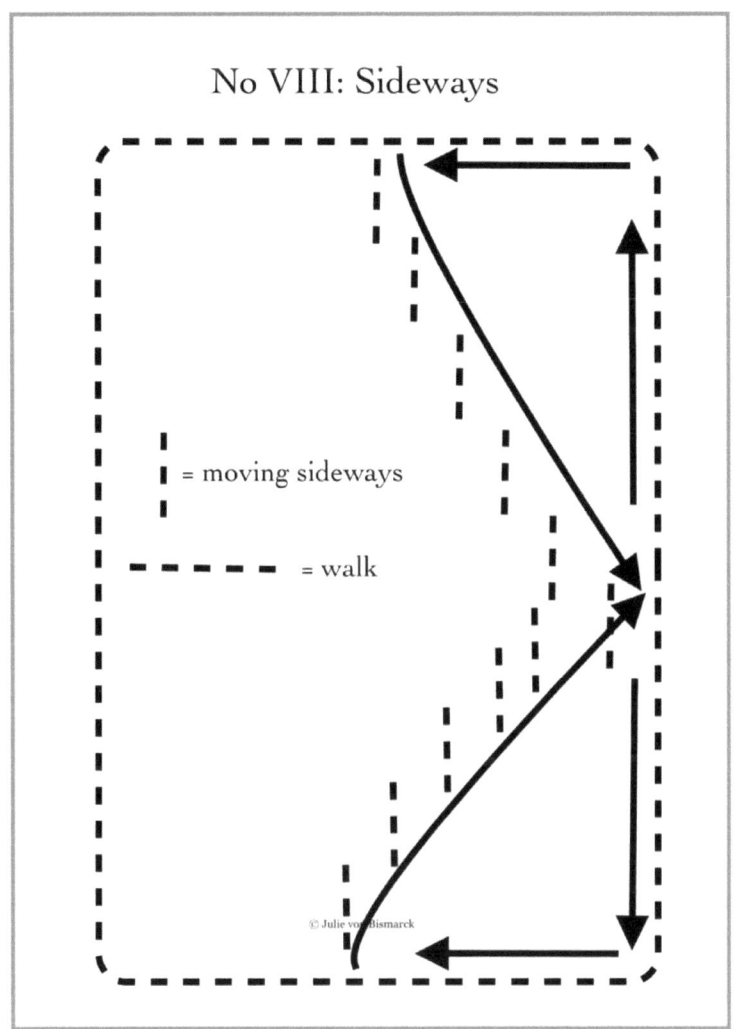

= moving sideways

= walk

© Julie von Bismarck

Exercise VIII: Sideways

Now that we've worked on fine coordination while riding straight and turning the shoulder, forehand and hindquarters, let's turn to the lateral movements.

The aim of this exercise is to make it quicker and easier for the horse to respond to the forward-sideways leg and weight aids, and to make the rider more aware of their own balance and uprightness, because almost nothing shows up seat errors and rider crookedness more clearly than (slow) lateral movements.
The exercise also mobilises the spines of both horse and rider.

It goes like this:
Go large around the track, riding in a brisk walk on a long rein. Before the short side, come down to a slow walk (without using the reins, as we've already learned), concentrating on each of the horse's steps as in Exercise I.
In the middle of the short side, turn onto the centre line and from there ride sideways back to the middle of the long side, changing the rein. Once on the track, ride on briskly straight ahead and repeat the whole sequence on the other rein.

The aim is to keep the horse as straight as possible in the lateral movement, i.e. not to flex or bend, but simply to move forward and sideways at a very slow walk.

The more stable and straighter your horse stays – especially in the neck – the better.

Imagine you are sitting on a four-legged plank and these four legs must now cross in such a way as to take you back to the track.

For this to work, it is essential to "close" the horse up: first take up the reins, keeping them long and of equal length (later you should be able to do this exercise without using the reins), turn your shoulders slightly in the direction of travel and look at the point where you want to end up. Make sure your hips don't turn too – remember that we always want to align our shoulders and hips as parallel to the horse's as possible, which almost always means that the hips and shoulders are doing opposite movements.

Example: You are riding a circle on the right rein. Your horse's left shoulder is further forward than its right. At the same time, though, its right hip is further forward than its left. For you, this means that you need to pull your right shoulder back and push your right hip forward.

I find it easier to imagine the movement as if you are pushing your outside shoulder and inside hip forward to the next level so that they "meet" on that level – while the inside shoulder and outside hip stay on the previous "neutral" level.

This process causes a rotation in your spine, so it only works well if the rider's spine is kept nice and mobile.

To help with this, I recommend various yoga and stretching exercises that are widely available (including some specially for riders).

By the way, this rotation takes place not only in the rider's spine but also (on a different –horizontal – level) in that of the horse.

Unfortunately, it is beyond the scope of this book to describe this in detail here, but I at least want to mention it so as to raise awareness once again that a horse that doesn't bend isn't necessarily "unrideable", but may simply be suffering from restricted mobility and pain in its back.

(If interested, you can read more about these links in my book *"Connections in the horse".*)

Back to our exercise:

Example: Ride in a brisk walk on the left rein, slow down the steps, turn onto the centre line by applying more pressure with your right knee/thigh so as to turn the horse's right shoulder. At the same time, use your right lower leg to make sure the horse's right hind leg steps properly into the front leg's tracks without deviating.

Use both legs to maintain forward momentum with the least possible pressure. Once on the centre line, ride three or four steps straight in walk and then turn your upper body slightly to the left.

And I do mean only slightly, down to around the 7th thoracic vertebra. Make sure to keep your hips/pelvis anchored very straight – the aim is to keep our horse as straight as possible.

Now use your left leg on the girth to drive your horse forward and take your right leg back slightly to move sideways. To keep the horse as straight as possible, I also recommend taking off the knee/thigh pressure and allowing both legs to rest as loosely as you can. This enables you to take corrective action at any time by realigning the horse's shoulders with the help of your right or left knee/thigh.

Think of it as aiming to have the horse's forehand, including neck and head, straight in front of you, and having the horse's legs cross underneath you, almost by the by and completely independently, without any flexion or bend.

Ride this exercise as slowly as possible, I really do mean in slow motion. You'll find this type of lateral movement much harder than, for example, a half-pass in trot, because as soon as the horse is flexed and bent, and certainly whenever the pace increases, small errors and shortcomings are very easy to conceal.

And that's exactly what we don't want – we're still working on focusing on the details.

If your horse takes the slow sideways movement as its cue to complete the rest of the walk sections at a leisurely pace as well, you can extend the brisk walk on a long rein by a long side in between, and wait for the opposite short side before starting the exercise again.

In fact, with every horse to which an easy, brisk, relaxed walk doesn't come easily, I recommend riding the exercise like this from the outset.

So once finished going sideways, walk forward on a long rein to the second short side, and only then turn back down the centre line.

Ask your horse for larger movements alternately with both legs, making sure you keep to a clear four-beat rhythm – i.e. if you notice your horse starting to hurry, bring it back into a slower action by moderating with your knees/thighs, shifting your centre of gravity slightly backwards and, if necessary, tensing your back.

So pin your ears back – but not too much, because by now your horse has learned to come down in response to this aid (Exercise I) so it may suddenly come to a standstill.

However, you will soon notice this and easily find the right "dosage" for your horse. Even though it may seem trivial, this takes you a huge step closer to fine riding and communication with your horse.

As with every exercise, ride this exercise evenly on both reins.

No IX: Thinking the Transition

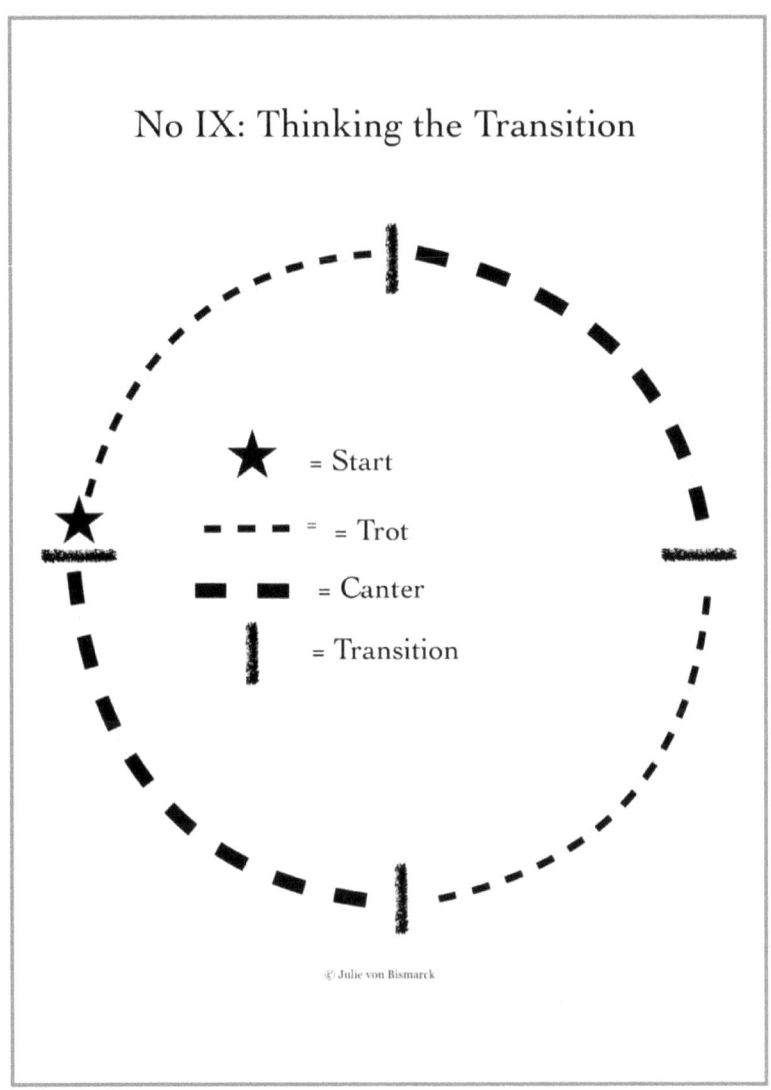

★ = Start

- - - = = Trot

■ ■ ■ = Canter

▌ = Transition

© Julie von Bismarck

Exercise IX: Thinking the Transition

This is the first of our exercises in which we add the canter. As some riders have more respect for this gait than for trot or walk, I'd like to start by saying a few words about it.

The canter is the gait in which a horse runs away.
Depending on the horse, the canter can become extremely fast and feel "uncontrolled".
There is sometimes a fine line between a canter that feels and actually is uncontrollable, because a cantering horse can spook at anything and take flight at any time, in other words: canter even faster.
If this is the case, the horse is acting in fight or flight mode and, as we've already seen, in this state the horse blanks out its surroundings, including the rider.

But this can happen just as easily from walk or trot.

In most cases, the idea that this danger is greater in canter is real only in the rider's mind.
However, many horses find a "slow" canter difficult at first, and this is not confined to young horses, because it can be equally true of an older horse if it hasn't learned and been schooled in a slow, controlled canter.

This, combined with an insecure rider, often does lead to the canter getting out of control and then, to make matters worse, many riders start to grip for fear of falling off – which understandably makes the horse go faster in turn.

So, before you start this exercise, be aware that your horse won't automatically run just because you go into canter.

Canter is a gait just like trot or walk, and just as normal a part of everyday training. Before picking up canter in this exercise, think about a slow-motion canter and matching your seat to it, staying calm and relaxed.

The aim of this exercise is to ride a flowing transition between canter and trot. In the end, the transition should be initiated by the rider simply thinking about the desired gait.

Like all of these exercises, this one is designed to increase the horse's attention to the rider's aids and to develop greater ease in riding. At the same time, it promotes suppleness and impulsion in the horse, and strengthens the abdominal muscles and with them the back and carrying power.

For all of these benefits to take effect, it is vital to do the exercise correctly. Ideally, the horse should start this exercise with a relaxed neck falling forwards from the withers and the nostrils always being the foremost point. If you have a horse that lifts its head and goes against the reins when going into canter, this will be the first main area you need to work on – but don't worry, this will settle after a few training sessions. (Provided your horse has no physical restrictions that cause problems in canter.)

Once the exercise is going well in a real forward-downward posture, it can also be ridden with more elevation and shorter intervals, in which case it serves to collect the horse.

It goes like this:
Ride on a large circle, beginning the exercise in trot. A rising trot is fine to start with. I usually prefer the centre circle but if you feel more comfortable cantering "into the short side" you can of course choose one of the other two circles.

The trot should be relaxed but not fast.
Now look for an exact point at which you want to canter, for example a specific point on the circle. Start thinking about the canter while still in trot, and straighten up by bringing tension to your stomach and upper body (your stomach will tend to "stick out" rather than be pulled in, maybe a new sensation for some of us...).
Allow your outside knee and thigh to rest against the horse with slight pressure and, with your outside lower leg slightly behind the girth, wrap your legs round the horse's belly (don't grip, just "contain"/put your legs on smoothly with a light pressure).

With the inside lower leg, now give the aid for canter; I call this "cantering from the inside leg".
To do this, take off the pressure from your inside thigh and knee (just the pressure, don't turn the knee/thigh out from the saddle), so as not to block the inside shoulder and forward reach of the front leg when picking up canter, and give an impulse with the inside lower leg.
Allow the outside leg to rest against the horse just as a guard, and canter at a steady pace using your inside leg.

Canter for six to eight strides, staying as relaxed as possible, and then calmly come back to trot. To do this, grip with your thighs/knees, pin your ears back and breathe out. To start with, of course, you can support the transition to trot with a half-halt on the reins, but the then hands should immediately go forward again to make space for the trot. After a quarter circuit of the track, pick up canter again as described above.

You can vary the number of canter strides and trot steps as you wish – depending on the horse, longer or shorter intervals may be better.

If you and your horse still have trouble with a steady canter, take your time to find the rhythm before coming back to trot – counting and keeping to the exact number of strides and steps can come later, there's no time pressure.

Try to imagine each canter stride as if it were actually happening in slow motion, and don't get flustered if your horse rushes at first or seems fast to you.

Keep stubbornly riding your chosen number of canter strides (this can be 10 or 12 or even 14) and imagine slowing the movement down with your thoughts.

To help your horse canter a bit more smoothly, it's important to sit as you would when moving with a very slow, steady canter.

Normally you would pick up canter again after a quarter circuit in trot, but if your horse is fizzy or hurries you can happily include up to a full circuit in steady trot to start with.

Crucially, don't try to brake in either canter or trot, just think about a steadier pace!

Braking by pulling on the reins and gripping with the legs tends to cause more tension/stress in the horse and our aim is to achieve a supple, relaxed, happy horse.

If you are riding a sluggish horse and having a real job to "keep the canter", I recommend reducing the number of canter strides and trot steps, i.e. transitioning more quickly between canter and trot. Trot a horse like this a bit more actively (not faster!) from the outset and give the canter aids with a little more body tension, i.e. with more emphasis overall.

In general, ride a horse like this with a high degree of tension in your own body – as opposed to a tense/hurrying horse, on which you have to sit as much like a "rag doll" as possible.

So increase your own muscle tone, sit for a few steps in trot before asking for canter, apply the outside leg as described earlier, but with more emphasis, and also give the impulse with your inside leg with more energy/emphasis than you would with a horse that tends to hurry.

With horses that have been "dull to the leg" like this for a while, it may be a good idea to take a whip with you for the first few training sessions. You can use the whip to support the leg aid (of the INSIDE leg!) with a quick tap. Most of the time, though, it's enough just to have it with you.

Canter for five or six strides, come back to trot, and pick up canter again after only five or so steps in trot. Repeat this until you notice that your horse responds immediately and canters on smoothly. Once this is the case, you can increase the number of canter strides, but I would keep this short trot interval.

Make the canter active, but not fast. You will need to come back to trot again immediately, so you can't use a fast pace.

It is astonishing to see how quickly "lazy" horses that their riders could keep in canter only with enormous effort and constant nagging suddenly pick up the canter eagerly and then maintain it in the same way.

For the rider, the main task is to concentrate on their seat and precise execution. Coming back to trot after exactly the set number of canter strides and cantering on again at precisely the set point is only possible with extreme concentration.

Don't expect it to work every time, and nor does it need to. If you can manage it a few times per session, you're already doing great.

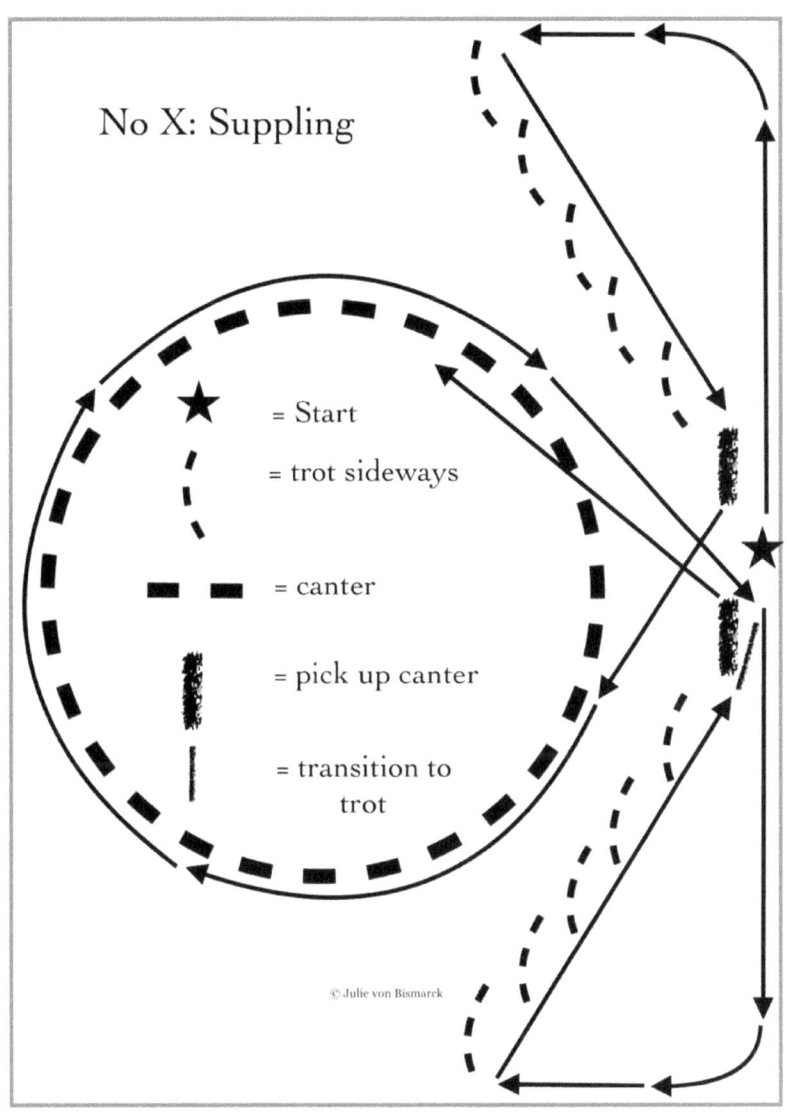

No X: Suppling

★ = Start

= trot sideways

= canter

= pick up canter

= transition to trot

© Julie von Bismarck

Exercise X: Suppling

The aim of the exercise is to ride an effortless transition between trot and canter and between two different bends.
This exercise demands quick reactions from the rider and is ideal for really getting the horse to become supple through its body.

It goes like this:
Go large around the track in sitting trot, nostrils the foremost point of the horse, horse in an upright, elevated position. As you come out of the corner, ride a half circle and back to the track, almost riding a little half-pass on the way, keeping your horse flexed and bent to the left on the left rein and to the right on the right rein, simply riding sideways.

Assuming you are riding on the left rein, this means: take the left flexion and bend with you into the half circle, use your right thigh and knee to turn the horse's right shoulder to the left, look at the point you want to reach on the track and imagine yourself walking along that line.

Now drive on with your left calf, take your left knee slightly off the horse, keep your horse flexed and bent to the left, and use your right thigh/knee and your resting, guarding right leg to push him left towards the track.

As you do this, of course, you also need to turn your shoulder girdle to the left so your shoulders remain parallel to those of the horse.

Make sure to keep your left hip in front; people often tend to move it as well and then there is a lack of driving momentum.

Try to manage with the least possible pressure – you can always use more if your horse doesn't respond.

Once at the track, you need to be quick: straighten your shoulders and hips as well as the horse again, flex the horse slightly to the right and pick up canter on the new inside leg (in this case your right leg) – as explained in the previous exercise. Ride straight to the centre circle, flex and turn your horse to the right and canter the circle once.

Concentrate on keeping your horse bent between your outside and inside leg and pulling your inside shoulder back and pushing your inside hip forward. If you find that tricky, try this:

Don't pull your inside shoulder back, but push your outside shoulder forward instead. And push the outside hip forward rather than pulling the inside hip back.

Many riders find this easier.

You may have to work a bit harder with the outside lower leg at times if, for example, you notice that the hindquarters are falling out. But in principle:

You ride steady, active canter strides, your inside leg stays long and drives into the movement, your outside leg limits, thigh and knee turn the horse's shoulder in the direction of travel, the lower leg guards and acts when necessary.

As always, the reins play only a minor role, as they are not the decisive aid here either.

As in all of these exercises:
You do of course have the reins in your hand, but imagine you are controlling your horse solely through your seat and with your legs.

And sit as passively and loosely as possible – you only need normal positive body tension for this exercise, so you can make your seat on the horse as relaxed as possible.

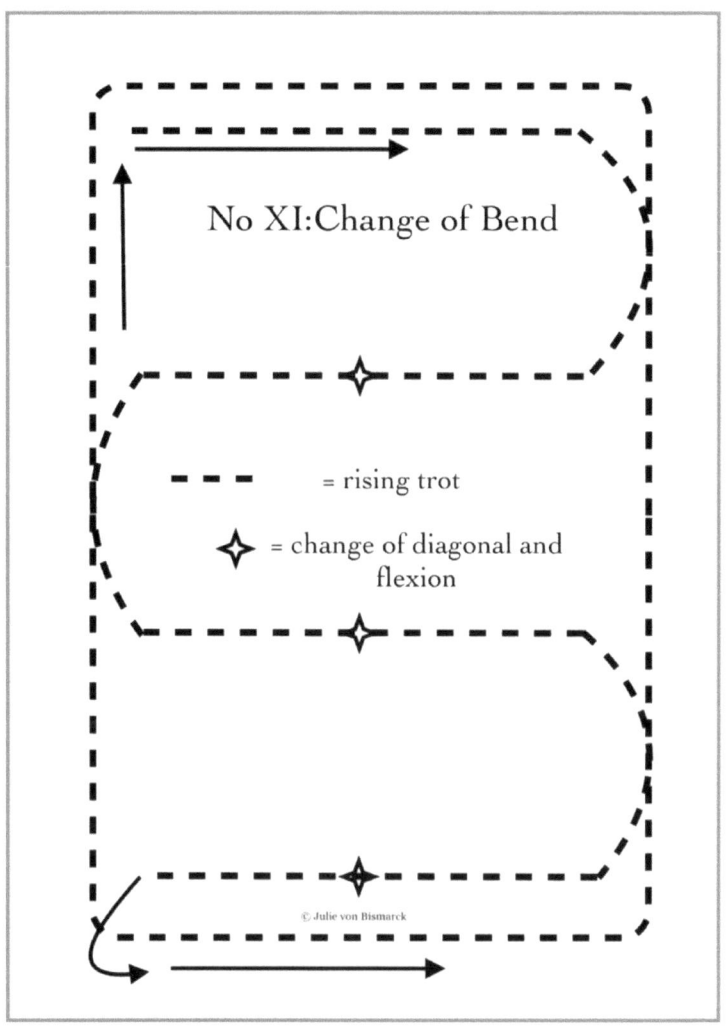

No XI:Change of Bend

--- = rising trot

✦ = change of diagonal and flexion

© Julie von Bismarck

Exercise XI: Change of Bend

This exercise effectively trains our concentration on the change between two different bends and flexions and a straight horse.
The exercise is also useful as part of a warm-up and requires quick thinking, acting and changes of diagonal.

It goes like this:
We are aiming to change the lead precisely in the middle of each line of the serpentine, not a step earlier or later.
I find it helps to put a jump stand at each spot first, which gives you a guide and makes it easier not to "cheat".

Make sure your horse is dead straight when you change the diagonal. As you're riding in flexion and bend just before and just after, this is not as easy as it sounds.

So go large around the track in rising trot, start the first line of your serpentine by making the second corner of the short side slightly rounder, make sure in the turn that the horse's forehand and hindquarters are aligned and that your shoulders and hips are parallel to those of the horse.
Drive on with your inside leg, use your outside knee/thigh to turn the forehand and use your outside leg to stop the horse's outside hind foot

154

from falling out.

As soon as you've completed the turn, straighten yourself and your horse, change diagonal and flex and bend your horse in the new direction.

Ride the exercise three times and then change the rein.

In this exercise we are aiming for a feeling that our horse is straightening and bending correctly solely in response to our seat, without pulling on the inside rein or "pushing" with the outside rein.

When horse and rider have figured this out, it feels as if the horse is merging with the rider's body and you are moving as one: wherever the horse's forehand goes, the rider's shoulders go, wherever the rider's pelvis is, the horse's pelvis goes, and vice versa.

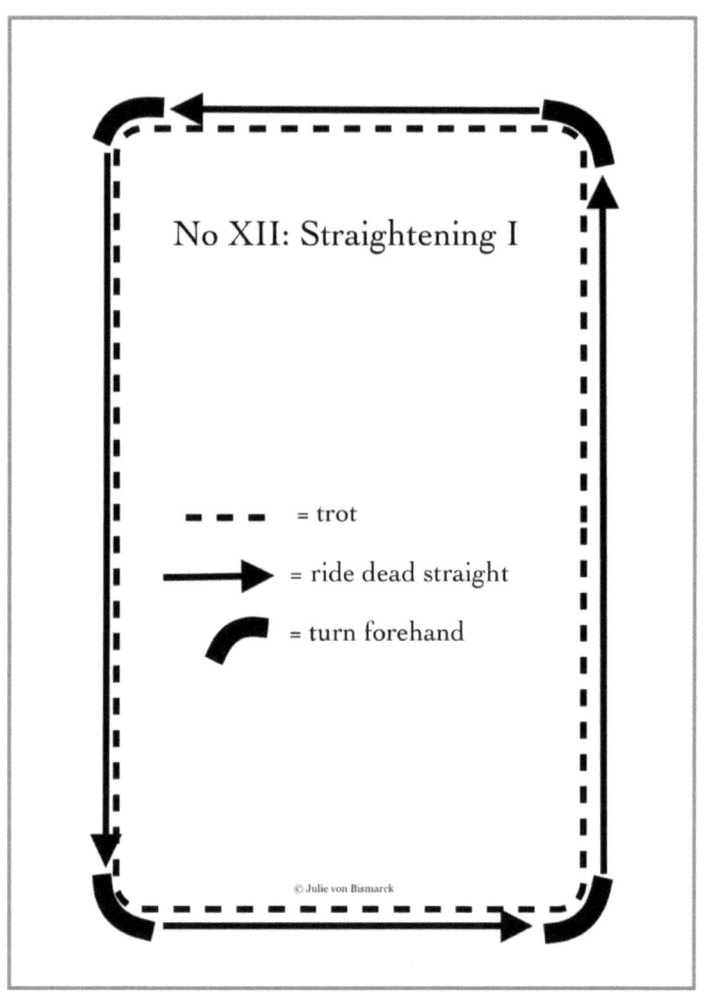

No XII: Straightening I

- - - = trot

→ = ride dead straight

= turn forehand

© Julie von Bismarck

Exercise XII: Straightening I

We have just practised riding straight along the short lines of a serpentine, and now we're aiming to practise it over a longer stretch.

Again, the exercise sounds easier than it is: we've already mentioned the natural crookedness or asymmetry of horse and rider – you'll find that riding a dead straight line is much easier said than done.

It definitely helps to build an alley out of poles to start with, but in the long run you should of course be able to do the exercise unaided.

The aim of the exercise is to have a dead straight horse under a dead straight rider, and to turn the forehand around the turn markers.

It goes like this:
Ride large around the second track in rising trot. Feel free to put jump stands in the four corners of this smaller track, so you know exactly where to turn.

Fix your eyes on a point at the other end of each straight line and aim directly for it. Imagine your shoulders and pelvis are fixed straight ahead, directly facing your point.

Don't worry about the horse's neck, leave the reins as long as possible and under no circumstances try to correct anything using the reins. In this exercise we're aiming to correct solely using our seat.

Drive on evenly with both legs, using as little pressure as possible. Your upper body should be tensed, your legs as relaxed as possible = neutral.

Now feel your horse's movement: is it falling out with a shoulder or a hind leg?
If so, here is your aid: keep your shoulders and pelvis pointing stubbornly straight ahead.
Correct the horse's shoulders by applying knee and thigh pressure on the side to which the shoulder wants to "escape".
Always start with the lightest possible pressure. Correct the hind legs with your same-side lower legs, again using as little pressure as possible at first.

Adjust the strength of the aid if necessary – but take the aid off again as soon as the horse responds and is straight again.
The moment the horse responds, your legs immediately go back to "neutral" = relaxed.
That is the key lesson in this exercise.

If you and your horse can master this interplay, you will both be a lot straighter. When starting out, have someone look from both front and back to see if you and your horse really are straight – this will help you memorise the right feeling.
At the corners, remember to turn only the forehand, keeping the horse as straight as possible, as if turning him straight around the jump stand.

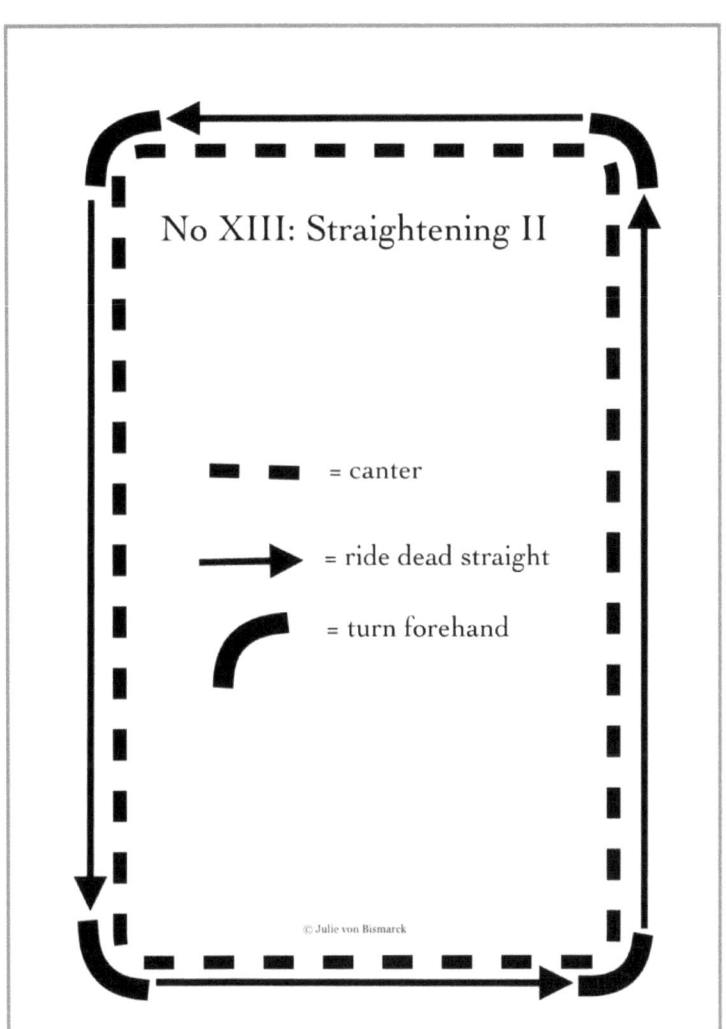

No XIII: Straightening II

= canter

= ride dead straight

= turn forehand

© Julie von Bismarck

Exercise XIII: Straightening II

Now we repeat the same exercise in canter. Here too, the aim of the exercise is to have a dead straight horse under a dead straight rider, and to turn the forehand around the jump stands.

It goes like this:
Ride large around the second track in a steady canter. Feel free to put jump stands in the four corners of this smaller track, so you know exactly where to turn.
Fix your eyes on a point at the other end of each straight line and aim directly for it. Imagine your shoulders and pelvis are fixed straight ahead, oriented directly towards your point.
Under no circumstances try to correct anything using the reins. In this exercise we are aiming to correct solely using our seat. Drive on as little as possible, keep the canter upright but try to do this with both legs equally if you can. Your upper body should be tensed, your legs as relaxed as possible = neutral.
Now feel your horse's movement: is it falling out with a shoulder or a hind leg? Is it hollowing? Which is common, especially in canter.

Your correction aids are essentially the same as those for the exercise in trot, just be even more careful to keep a relaxed seat on the horse, as many riders tend to grip in canter.

But that would prevent you from correcting your horse. So stay relaxed, ride at a steady pace, keep your shoulders and pelvis pointing stubbornly straight ahead, and correct the horse's shoulders in the usual way by applying pressure from the same-side knee and thigh.

Always start with the lightest possible pressure.

Correct the hind legs with your same-side lower legs, again using as little pressure as possible at first.

Adjust the strength of the aid if necessary – but take the aid off again as soon as the horse responds and is straight again.

The moment the horse responds, your legs go back to "neutral" = relaxed. That is the key lesson in this exercise.

If your horse has already learned flying changes, focus on not taking your lower leg too far back when correcting the hind leg and on pushing the horse more into the straight line between both legs.

When starting out, have someone look from both front and back to see if you and your horse really are straight – this will help you memorise the right feeling.

At the corners, remember to turn only the forehand, keeping the horse as straight as possible, as if turning him straight around the jump stand, or ride a quarter pirouette – just without the flexion and bend.

This exercise can also be done in open country. All you need is a sense of what it should feel like when the horse really is straight – and a long field or track.

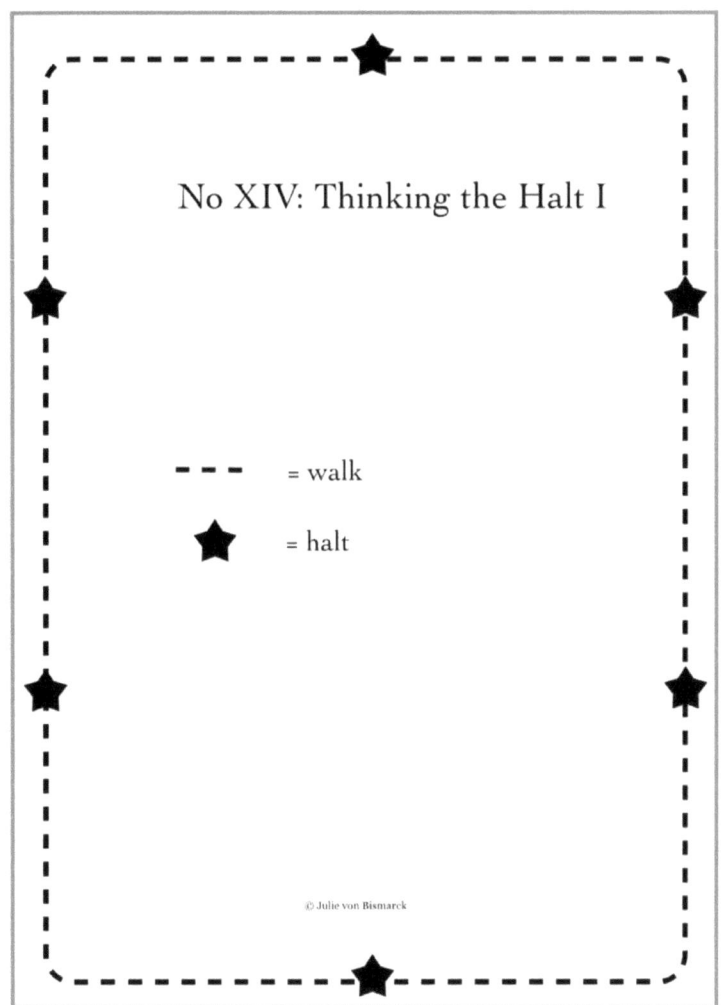

No XIV: Thinking the Halt I

- - - = walk

★ = halt

© Julie von Bismarck

Exercise XIV: Thinking the Halt I

The aim of this exercise is to refine communication in the halt and to master halting without using the reins.

The benefits extend to reducing speed within a gait, because it trains the rider's feeling for making the horse slow down or speed up with concentration and the resulting body tension. As in Exercise I, the aim here is to manage as far as possible without using the reins and to control the horse solely through focus and seat.

It goes like this:
Go large around the track in walk, leaving the reins long. Halt in the middle of each short side and at the two circle points on the long sides, make the horse stand for a few seconds, and then ride on. As you approach each halt, imagine controlling your horse's last few steps through your seat, feel your sitting bones, tense your stomach and pelvic floor, and grip a bit more with your thighs.
Think: slow => even slower => slow motion => stop.

This gets your horse ready for halt. To halt, pin back your ears, grip with your knees, breathe out and think "haaaaalt". Feel free to say this out loud. Voice aids are a great tool for communication with the horse, especially when just starting out in this style of riding. You just need to use them precisely and you definitely shouldn't talk constantly to the horse.

Be careful about halting at the exact points, no earlier and no later.

Ask your horse for a relaxed walk in between the halt points, taking the "control" from your pelvic floor/back and stomach and relaxing your seat to follow the horse's movements.

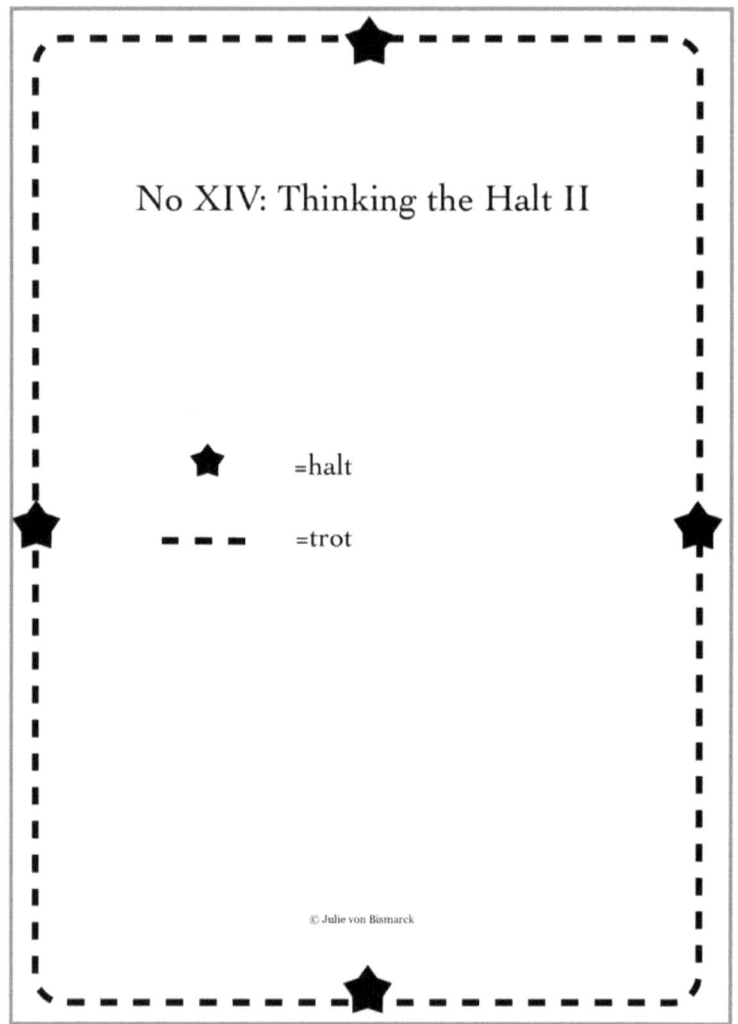

No XIV: Thinking the Halt II

★ =halt

- - - =trot

© Julie von Bismarck

Exercise XV: Thinking the Halt II

Now we take the coordination worked on in the previous exercise into the trot. This exercise has the same goal as part I and later will be ridden in canter as well (making it part of the exercises for advanced riders) but in trot it is suitable for every rider and every horse.

To make it easier for us and our horse, we should always have ridden part I of the exercise first – this makes sure we both already know what it's about. By the way, I find it easier to ride this exercise without stirrups at first, but you can try that out for yourself.

It goes like this:
Go large around the track in a steady sitting trot. Later on you can also try the exercise in rising trot, sitting for two steps before halting. Leave the reins long – it's not about elevation or contact (though this is of course allowed), but mainly about getting the horse to halt from trot and to trot on again from halt using only your seat.

Precisely in the middle of each short side and long side, come down to halt without using the reins. As in the version in walk, think: slower => slow motion => stop.
Don't think walk, just think slow trot and halt. The slower you trot at the start, the easier it is for you

and your horse to put the exercise into practice. Later on you can also ride the exercise from an active trot.

Imagine your horse coming straight to a halt from trot. In the last few steps, tense your pelvic floor, back and stomach again and hug the horse more with your thighs.

The halt aid is then the same as for any halt: breathe out, pin back your ears, grip with your knees.

If it doesn't work right away, don't worry, you have plenty of time. Don't be discouraged if your horse doesn't stand right away. Use your voice and, crucially, give your horse lots of praise when it stops for the first time, and maybe a treat. You'll see how quickly your horse stands at the next halt. In fact, I give a treat after every halt the first time a horse rides this exercise. After that, "normal" praise will have to do.

Make the horse stand for around two seconds (longer with treats, of course) and trot on again. The horse's very first movement should be a trot step, so think trot and imagine coming out of the halt straight into an active trot again. Increase your overall body tension to bring tension to the horse and give a strong squeeze with both calves, tensing your stomach and pelvic floor as well.

When riding a horse that has switched off due to its previous training, we have to be careful not to grip with the legs. With a horse like this it's especially important to make sure you have a loose, relaxed leg that works only by giving impulses.

In this case it's best to apply both legs briefly and give an impulse with the calf. If there is no immediate response, apply the lower legs one by one: once inside, once outside, using more pressure and alternating quickly.

Normally this shouldn't be necessary at this point in the exercise series, but some horses associate "halt" with a slightly more leisurely inner attitude and these horses tend to cheat their way into trot via walk.
But this is not the aim of the exercise, so it is better to apply the whip again behind the inside calf rather than to grip with the legs.

No XVI: The miracle of fine riding I

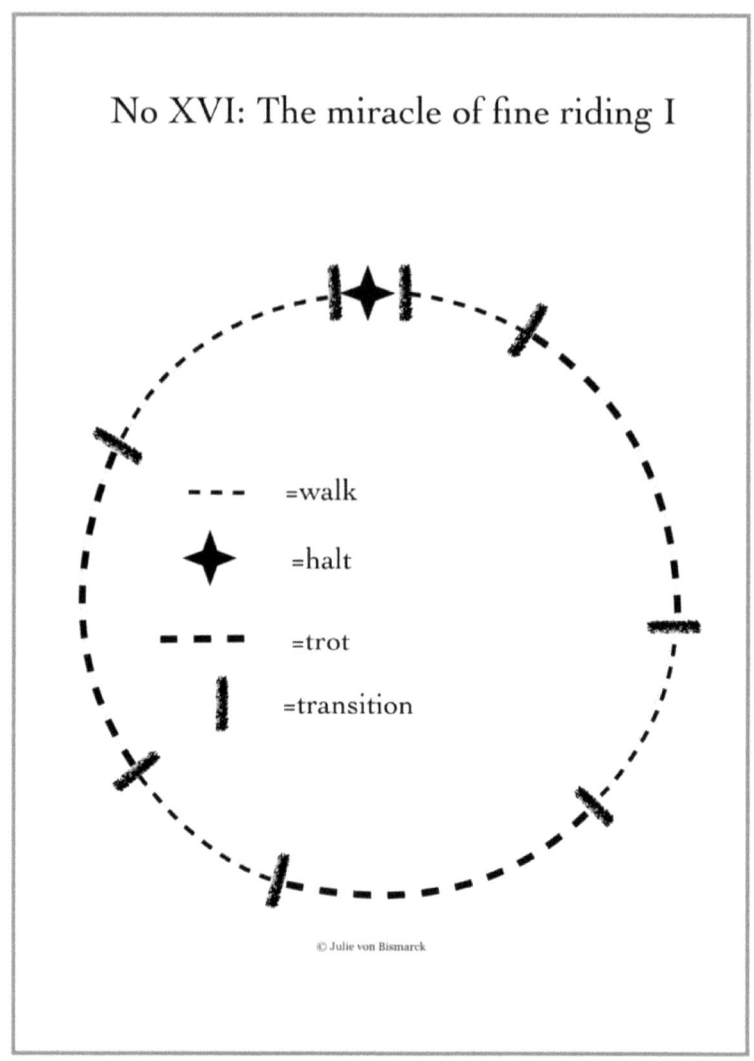

--- =walk

✦ =halt

- - - =trot

| =transition

© Julie von Bismarck

Exercise XVI: The Miracle of Fine Riding I

You probably remember our Exercise I – Find the Feet, with which we started this training series. What we worked on in that first exercise, and refined in the last two exercises, we will now develop further by taking the whole thing from a straight line to a curve and transitioning between three phases: walk, halt and trot.

The aim of the exercise is to have a correctly bent horse that transitions smoothly from one gait to the next and comes down to a halt in response to invisible aids.

It goes like this:

Ride in walk on the circle. I like to use the centre circle for this, but to start with you can also use a circle that is visually limited to three sides along one of the short sides.

Our horse is already warmed up, for example by doing Exercises I to IV or simply by warming up along curved and straight lines.

Stop at A or C (B or E if riding the centre circle) and make the horse stand still for three seconds. Then ride off in walk and count 8 – 10 steps. On the 8th step think trot, by the 9th or 10th step at the latest transition to trot. As in Exercise I, the transition should be smooth and fluid and the trot slow enough that we can consciously count each step.

After precisely 10 trot steps, transition back to walk in the same way that we worked on in Exercise I, without using the reins.

Vary the number of steps in walk between 3 and 10, i.e. 3 steps one time, 7 the next time, and so on, and then trot on again. It's important to decide the number of steps beforehand and then to keep to them exactly. You can also announce them out loud; some riders find this helps.

Continue like this until you reach the halt point again and try to reach it alternately from walk and trot then riding on in the same gait, as we saw in the previous exercises. The transitions between gaits and halt should be smooth and effortless. To do this, try to keep your seat as loose and relaxed as you can. Bear in mind that this exercise should require almost no effort and you want to ride your transitions as "un-jerkily" as possible.

Make sure to align your shoulders and hips as they should be when the horse is moving correctly bent on the circle. This will also make it easier for your horse to walk in the correct bend.

So take your inside shoulder back – or the outside one forward if that's easier for you – and push your inside hip forward.

Riding on a circle, the horse's inside hind leg walks a smaller track than the outside hind leg, so its hip bone reaches further forward, which means that your inside hip or pelvic bone – I think that's easier to visualise – should do that too.

To stop the horse's outside shoulder coming off the circle, we adjust the pressure from our outside knee/thigh accordingly, limiting the shoulder.
We use our lower legs to correct the hind legs if necessary.

Keep in mind that the halt happens on a curve too, which means that the inside hind leg can stand a little further in and the forehand is also curved. Only slightly of course, but as we saw at the beginning, riding is all about these tiny differences. Imagine how your horse should look from above when standing on a circle line and try to halt exactly like that.

No XVII: The miracle of fine riding II

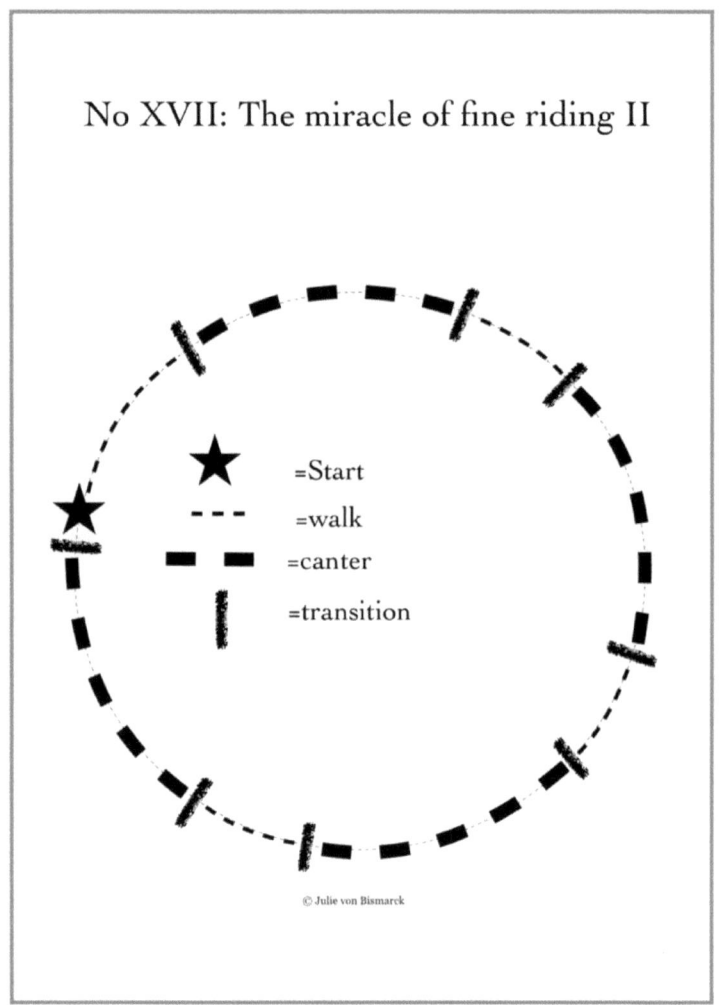

★ =Start

- - - =walk

▬ ▬ =canter

| =transition

© Julie von Bismarck

Exercise XVII: The Miracle of Fine Riding II

To start with, we always ride this second part of the exercise directly after the first part. Once the fine tuning is established, it can also be ridden individually.

This exercise brings together all the previous steps on the theme of "walking on, coming back and halting in response to the finest of aids" and allows us to reap the benefits of what we and our horse have worked on through all the other exercises.
Especially if you have a previously "sluggish", "jaded" horse, you'll be delighted when this exercise works for the first time.

It goes like this:
Ride in walk on the circle and look for a starting point. From this point, count exactly 8 steps in walk and then pick up canter on the inside leg. After 5 canter strides, come back to walk; continue like this for 1–3 circuits, then change the rein.
Keep a slight connection to the horse's head (except of course if riding on a neck ring or with nothing at all), count the steps and think of canter at the 7th step at the latest.
Imagine the horse immediately pushing off from the hindquarters, rising to meet you and then taking exactly 5 strides in canter.
It's very important to think about the limited number of strides right away, because it's pretty

short and from the very first stride you'll need to concentrate on slowing down to walk again while controlling the canter.

To this end, keep the tension in your body and keep the horse very controlled between your legs. So lots of knee grip, thighs on the horse, lower legs in smooth contact too.

You and your horse need positive tension to perform the exercise. For once, maintain this tension in a slightly weaker version during the walk phases of the exercise.

Normally we try to bring as little tension as possible into the horse in walk, but in this case we need it.

Alternate between canter and walk on the circle in this way, but never ride more than three circuits on each rein.

Even if it's a lot of fun: experience shows that you can quickly overdo this exercise and horses can become "fizzy", over-eager or crooked. Personally, I call it a day as soon as the horse and I have managed 2 or 3 really good, fluid transitions with immediate response – and I would recommend that you do the same.

Now ride a few circuits in forward-downward trot to get the tension back out of the horse. If you are new to this exercise, I would recommend that you include it at the end of your session and then call it a day.

Later on, you can use it anywhere and it's also a great exercise to ride in open country.

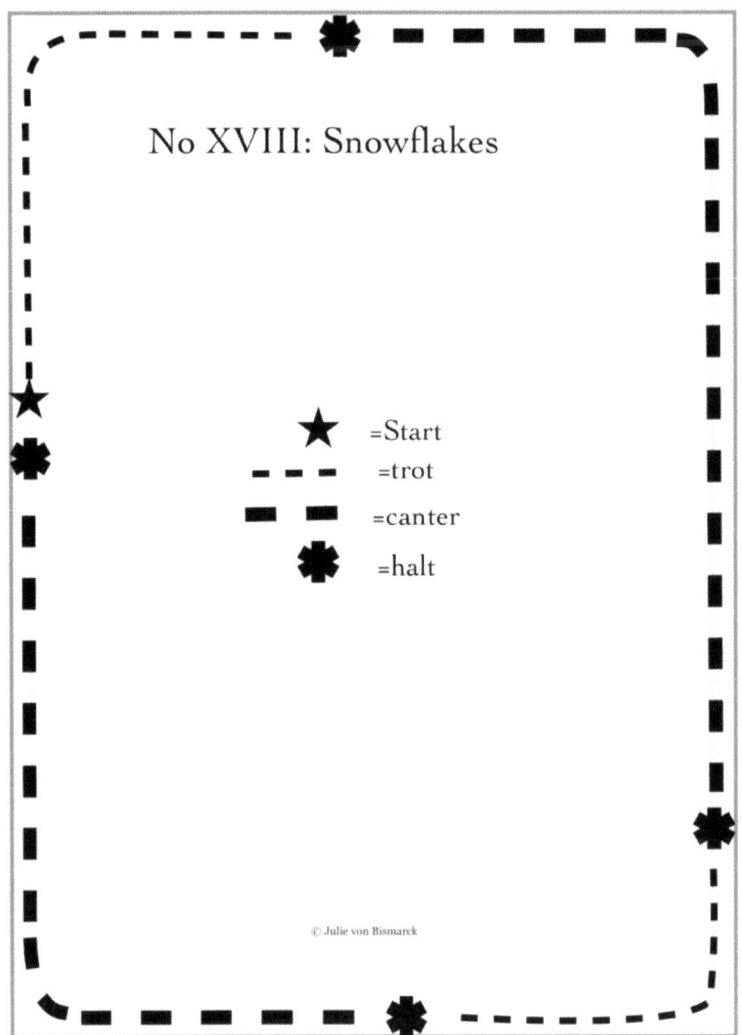

No XVIII: Snowflakes

★ =Start
--- =trot
▬ ▬ =canter
✳ =halt

© Julie von Bismarck

Exercise XVIII: Snowflakes

With this newfound ease in communication between ourselves and our horse, we now go a step further and transition between trot, canter and halt to further refine our aids.

In the previous exercise, the horse soon realised that we were only transitioning between walk and canter, so it knew what was coming. Here, things get trickier and rider and horse really need to concentrate.

It goes like this:

Start in the middle of the long side and pick up sitting trot. In the middle of the short side, halt as described in the previous exercises.

Make the horse stand briefly, maintaining your body tension, and tell the horse that you are about to canter from halt. Do this by giving an impulse with your inside calf and guarding with your outside calf, as we saw earlier.

Inside leg asks for canter, outside leg guards. Put your thighs on without gripping, keeping tension in your stomach and upper body. Ride in a controlled but active canter, imagining your horse growing taller in front of you, and make sure to control its shoulders and hind legs with your legs if the horse goes crooked. (See exercise "Straightening".)

Before the corner, think about a shorter, slower canter and come down smoothly into trot (as always, without using the reins if possible). Think about the first trot step as soon as you start slowing down!

In the middle of the short side, halt again and canter again from the halt.
If this is easy and working well, you can vary the exercise: change the number of canter strides, canter a whole circuit in between, trot 5 steps, 10 steps, a whole long side, and halt at a different point.

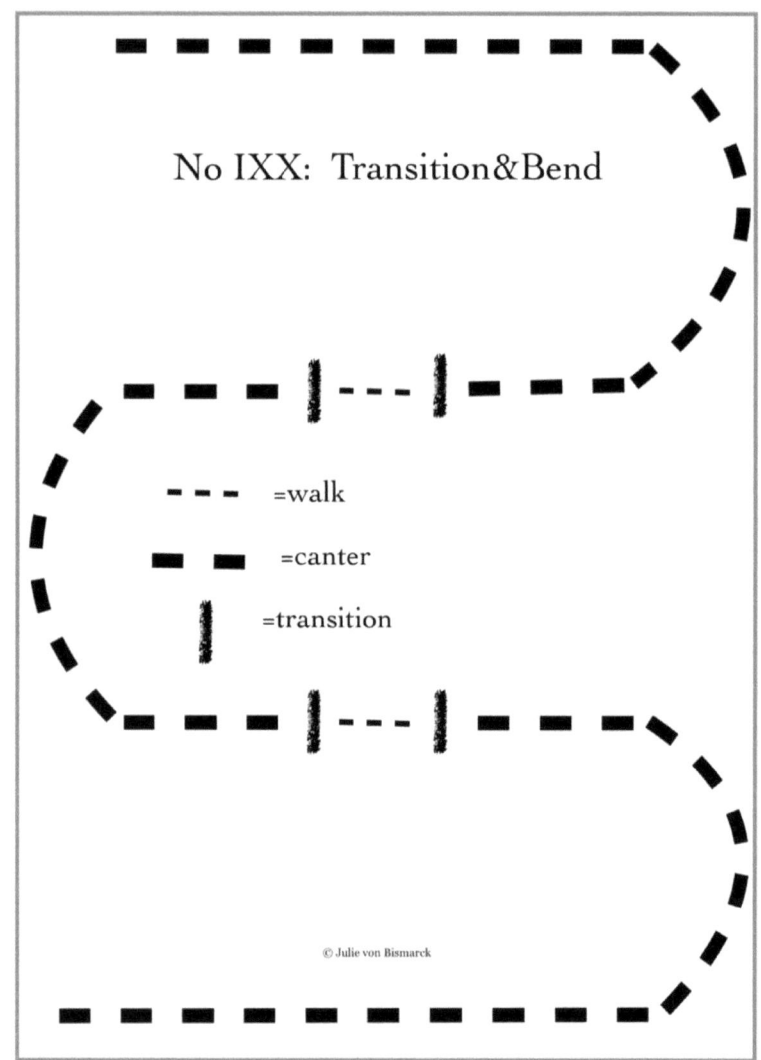

No IXX: Transition&Bend

- - - =walk

■ ■ =canter

=transition

© Julie von Bismarck

Exercise IXX: Transition and Bend

In this exercise we add several new challenges: alternating between bends, between canter and walk, and between canter right and canter left.

It goes like this:
Go large around the track and pick up a steady but active canter. In the middle of the short side, begin a serpentine by riding the corner a little rounder and turning towards the centre line.

Start thinking now about the transition to walk because, depending on the size of the canter stride, this will come fairly quickly after the turn.

Aim to be in walk before the centre line. After three steps in walk, canter again on the new rein.
To start with, I recommend putting a jump stand at the transition to walk and another at the place where you're going to canter – this helps the rider to focus precisely on that spot and to communicate as accurately as possible with the horse.

Let's assume you start on the right rein: ride a steady right canter into the short side, before the corner turn the horse's outside shoulder with your outside knee/thigh, drive on with your inside leg and keep the outside calf tightly on the horse.

This exercise too calls for constant positive body tension to ensure fast responses.

Coming out of the turn, point your shoulder and pelvis straight ahead again, think about cantering slower, slow motion, backwards and only then think about walk, transition to walk for three steps, keeping tension in your stomach and pelvic floor, on the second step turn your shoulder in the new direction of travel (to the left) and push your left pelvic bone forward slightly.

On the third step, think about cantering left and the fourth step is the first canter stride. Ask for this by giving an impulse with your inside (left) calf and applying pressure with your outside (right) thigh and knee.

The outer calf comes back in guarding position. Now ride into the left turn and carry on.

Important: when riding this exercise, you and your horse should have fully mastered all of the previous exercises, and the horse must have learned to carry itself and to manage with only a very light rein contact (if any). In this exercise we don't want to turn using the reins or come back to walk.

The reins are just there to assist our body's actions and our focus.

If you don't bear this in mind, you may find that this exercise turns out the way it's ridden in many German and international dressage competitions at medium level: a lot of tugging and spurring to achieve a simple change of leg in canter.

So it's essential to think about a smooth transition from one gait to another, and don't be distracted by the fact that there are so many things to consider all at the same time.

Repeat the sequence over and over in your mind – you'll notice how easy it suddenly becomes to complete the exercise correctly:

canter, canter, turn, canter, canter slower, canter backward, into walk, change diagonal, change bend, pick up canter on the new inside leg.

And you won't be the first rider to cause jaws to drop at the stables because an exercise so dreaded and disliked by others suddenly looks so easy and flowing when done by you and your horse.

No XX: The Diamond

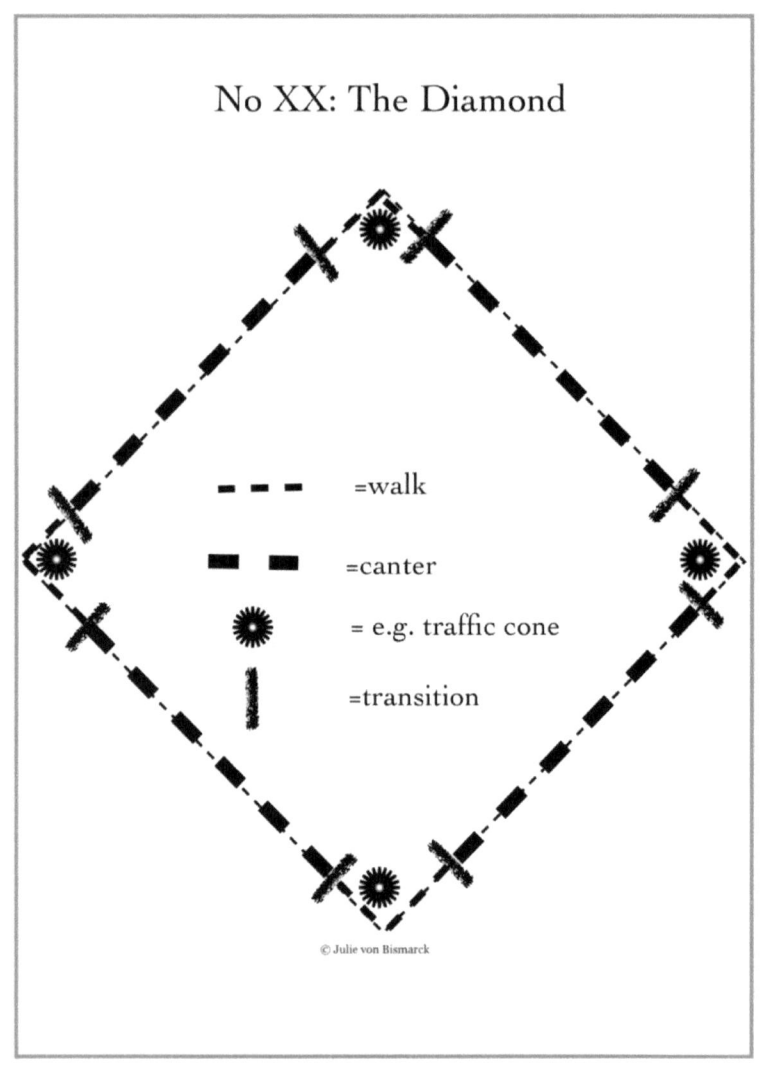

- - - =walk

■ ■ =canter

✻ = e.g. traffic cone

| =transition

© Julie von Bismarck

Exercise XX: The Diamond

This exercise is very demanding for rider and horse and should therefore be attempted only if all of the previous exercises are going well without really using the rein aids.

It involves transitioning between canter, walk and a quarter pirouette, as well as the results of the "straightening" exercise, and is ideal for getting the horse on the hindquarters and freeing up the forehand.

This exercise is one of the best preparations for collecting lessons and once again improves the concentration and communication of rider and horse on a completely different level.

It goes like this:
Set up four jump stands in the shape of a diamond or tilted square. Make the shape as large as possible to begin with.

Start by riding around it a few times in walk on both reins, turning around each jump stand with a quarter pirouette. (See exercise "The Square".)

If this goes well, pick up canter.
Ride a very steady canter in this exercise too, as this will make it easier for you and your horse to come down into walk.

Just before each turn, come down to walk as in Exercise XIX, but here it is especially important to think of the horse as being completely straight again. Both in canter and in the transition to walk, the horse should feel stable and straight beneath you.

Now turn the horse's forehand around the jump stand from walk as described in Exercise VI. When you reach the next side of the square, pick up canter again.

Ride this exercise no more than 3 times on each rein and, if you can, try setting up the jump stands in a field or large meadow and riding the exercise there.

PS: You can also use the jump stands you've put up to vary the exercise a little: in this variation, ride in trot on the tilted square – you can use a steady rising trot – and turn the horse's forehand at each jump stand without flexing the horse. Try to imagine your horse staying straight even in the turn (which of course it isn't) just as it is straight on the sides of the square, as this helps to really turn the outside shoulder.

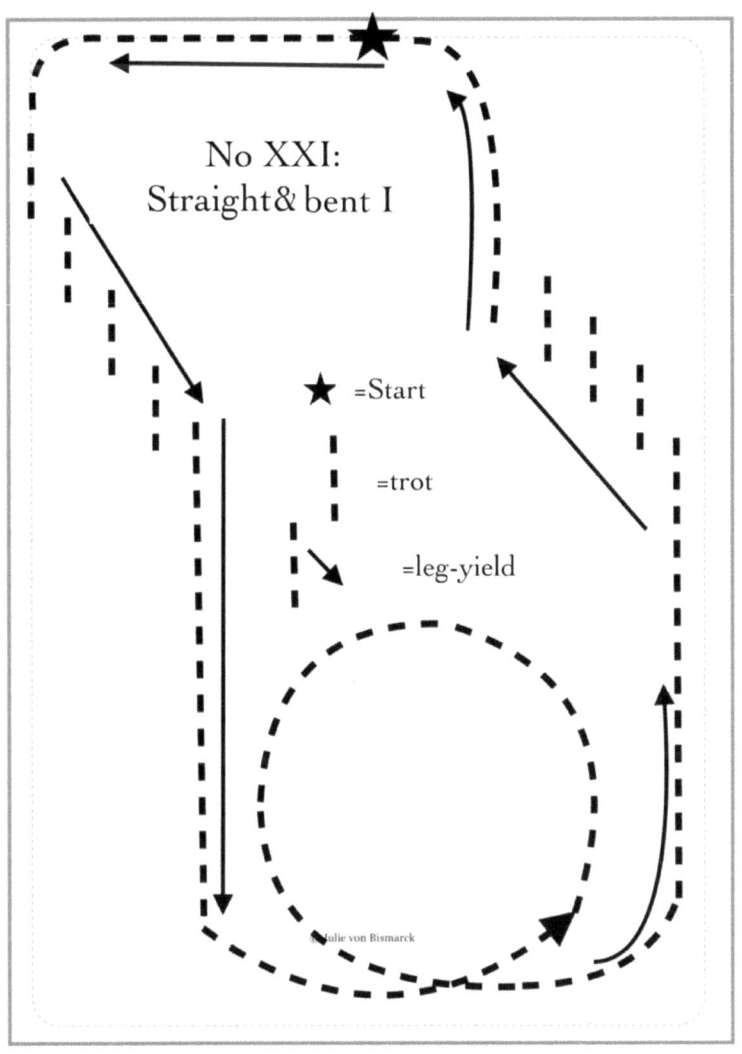

No XXI:
Straight& bent I

★ =Start

=trot

=leg-yield

Julie von Bismarck

Exercise XXI: Straight and Bent I

In this exercise we focus on the change between a straight horse and a horse on a curved line. You can also ride part I of this exercise after Exercise VIII.

It goes like this:

Go large around the track in trot, either rising trot or sitting trot is fine.

At the start of the long side, leg-yield the horse away from the rail to approximately the quarter line. As you do this, keep the horse and your pelvis fairly straight, turn your shoulders and pelvis only slightly inwards and look in the direction you want to ride. The inside calf drives on, while the outside calf pushes the horse sideways.

Once at the quarter line, ride straight ahead to the short side, turn and ride straight into a circle.

For the transition from "riding dead straight" to riding on a curved line, put more weight on your outside thigh/knee, leave your outside calf on the horse, give the horse's inside shoulder some room by taking your inside knee off slightly, and drive forward with your inside calf.

Coming out of the circle, ride back to the track and straighten yourself and the horse, then leg-yield inwards again from the rail, at the quarter line ride straight forward again and then turn again at the short side on the same rein to repeat the exercise.

Repeat the exercise five times on each rein.

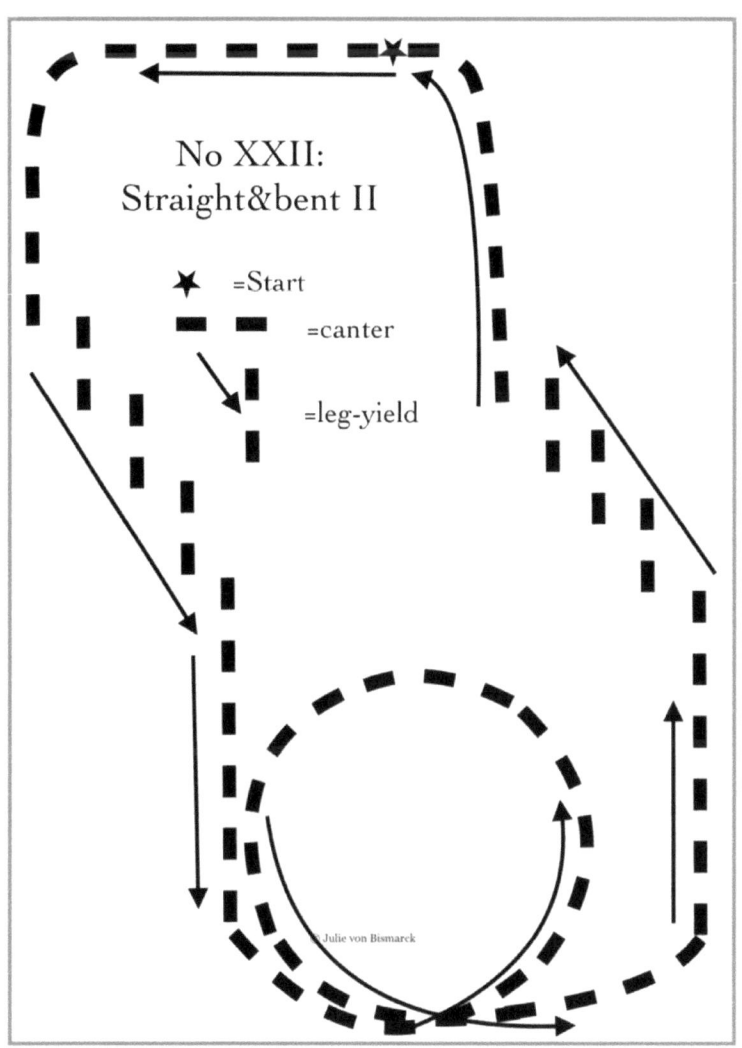

No XXII:
Straight&bent II

★ =Start

=canter

=leg-yield

© Julie von Bismarck

Exercise XXII: Straight & Bent II

In the second part of this exercise, we ride the same thing in canter. Go large around the track in a steady, controlled, easy canter.

At the start of the long side, move the horse sideways and inwards to the quarter line, keeping the horse as straight as possible.

Look in the direction you want to ride, but otherwise think "straight" rather than "sideways" and keep your seat relaxed.

Push your horse inwards with your outside leg and then canter on straight again.

Once on the quarter line, take the pressure off the outside calf, make sure the horse is straight between both legs again as if pulled on a string, and ride forward to the short side.

Slightly shorten the two canter strides before reaching the short side, so you can ride into the circle without your horse skidding.

In the circle, use your outside knee/thigh to turn the horse's shoulder, taking your inside shoulder back and your inside pelvic bone forward. Inside calf drives, outside calf limits.

Ride out of the circle, back to the track, straighten yourself and the horse again and at the start of the long side shift towards the quarter line again.

Once at the short side, turn again on the same rein as described in part I.

If you notice your horse "dropping out" in canter, having problems with balance or starting to hurry, ride a whole circuit of the track in between, maybe change to trot briefly and then try again.

PS: Most riders and horses find this exercise easier in canter.

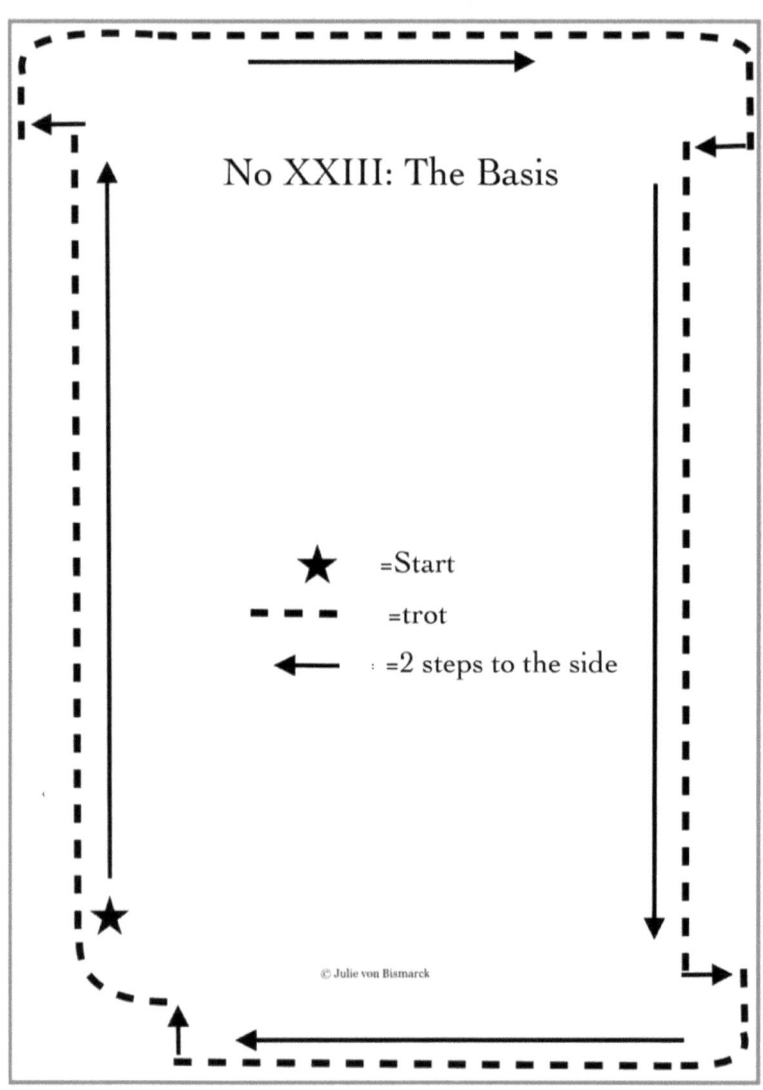

No XXIII: The Basis

★ =Start

▪▪▪ =trot

← =2 steps to the side

© Julie von Bismarck

Exercise XXIII: The Basis

I could have put this exercise right at the very start, but I saved it for last.

This is one of the exercises that have given me the fastest and most impressive successes in training the attention of rider and horse, but also in schooling the horse's movements.
This exercise works wonders, especially for horses that tend to step wide behind.

At the same time, it is the absolute basic exercise for every horse and rider and I would include it in every warm-up (if ridden in the arena).
The exercise trains the rider's responsiveness and concentration and immediately starts a lively conversation between horse and rider.

It goes like this:
Go large around the track in rising trot, riding on the second track on the long side.
Just before the corner, make your horse step sideways (in trot) to the outside so that it ends up on the first track. As you do this, keep your horse straight or slightly flexed inwards and imagine you want to send the horse's hindquarters forward, otherwise your horse may not cross behind and then the benefit of the exercise is lost.

Once on the first track, ride deep into the first and second corner on the short side.

Immediately after reaching the long side, make your horse take another step to the inside so that you are back on the second track, and so on.

Make sure to use the aids from the "Straightening" exercise on the long sides and really keep your horse "on the string".

For the sideways step, increase your body tension, apply both thighs more firmly on the horse and push it sideways with the appropriate leg. So one time inside leg, the next time outside leg, then inside leg again.

Concentrate on not trying to correct or influence with the reins, and when riding the corners, push your inside hip forward and take your inside shoulder back and straighten again immediately after the corner.

Look in the mirror or ask someone on the ground to check that you and your horse are completely straight on the long sides and that the horse really does cross when stepping sideways.

If you are riding a horse that steps wide behind, ask someone to check if the footing changes – this happens in most horses after a few repeats.

There are, of course, many other exercises that are excellent for refining communication with the horse. But as the scope of this book is limited, I have chosen a selection of exercises that should be easy to follow for any horse/rider pairing and that, in my experience, are especially helpful for both horse and rider, especially when starting to change their riding style.

I hope that this style of schooling will give you as many new insights and as much pleasure as it has given me and that you will deepen your friendship with your horse and hopefully feel you understand your horse even better by doing this kind of work.
I hope that you will experience how easy riding can be, how a seemingly dull horse suddenly becomes eager and responds to the smallest aids and gestures, or how a horse that is always tense suddenly lets go and listens as a result of this kind of quiet, friendly and easy communication.

In short: I hope that you will experience and understand how loud it can be when you whisper.

And that this volume is perfectly loud enough to have a conversation with the horse, despite its size and strength.

Julie von Bismarck

More books by Julie von Bismarck:

Reitsport – Auf dem Rücken des Pferdes

Equestrian sport - On the horse´s back

Zusammenhänge im Pferd

Connections in the horse

Zusammenhänge im Pferd II

Connections in the horse II

Reeva und die Pferde – Sommer auf Gut Balmore

Reeva and the horses - Summer on Balmore estate

Content